IMAGE CONSULTING FOR THE 21ST CENTURY

ꬲꬲꬲꬲꬲꬲ

Brenda York McDaniel
with Carol Caviezel Pardon

Published by the Academy of Fashion & Image

What Do You Want To Know About Image Consulting?

FOR PROSPECTIVE IMAGE CONSULTANTS

What is image consulting <u>really</u> like?
Is it right for me?
Where can I get the training I need to become certified?

FOR BEGINNING IMAGE CONSULTANTS

What do I need to do to set up shop?
How much should I charge?
How can I attract a clientele right away?

FOR ESTABLISHED IMAGE CONSULTANTS

What's new for the profession in the 21st century?
What are effective ways to expand my customer base?
How can I improve my business and marketing savvy?

THE ANSWERS
—AND MUCH MORE—
ARE IN THIS BOOK.

Published by
Academy of Fashion & Image
19860 N. 85th Ave.
Peoria, AZ 85382

Library of Congress Catalog Card Number: 00-191689

ISBN No. 0-9703595-0-0

Printed in the United States of America

ACKNOWLEDGMENTS

- I want to express my gratitude

  - first, to the book's co-author, Carol Caviezel Pardon, my dear friend and business consultant for 20 years;

  - second, to my son, Peter Petro, Jr., who always provides love, encouragement, and support for my work in the image industry;

  - third, to my husband, Derald McDaniel, the love and light of my life.

- I extend special thanks to Veronika Barnes for editing and proofing, to Dorothea James for editing and counsel, and to Lillian Johnson, who has provided friendship, advice, and much support.

- Thank you to the many friends and associates who have encouraged and supported this endeavor.

- Finally, I want to thank the graduates of AFI. It is because of you that the Academy of Fashion & Image exists. It is because of you that I founded the Association of Fashion & Image Consultants, and because of you that this book was written. You have truly been a source of inspiration and strength.

CONTENTS

ACKNOWLEDGEMENTS   v

INTRODUCTION   x

1.   HISTORY OF THE IMAGE INDUSTRY   1
      *Evolution of the image consulting business from the 1960s through
      the 1990s.*

2.   WHY CHOOSE IMAGE CONSULTING AS A CAREER?   13
      *Advantages and challenges of image consulting. A representative
      sampling of students and why they are going into the profession.
      Industry observations and predictions from practicing image
      consultants.*

3.   WHAT IT TAKES TO BE AN IMAGE CONSULTANT   35
      *Personal characteristics, background, education, training, and other
      requisites for success as an image consultant.*

4.   GETTING STARTED   47
      *What you need to know to get started in image consulting, including
      the business side, identifying and developing a clientele, marketing,
      and what to charge. Plus real-life success stories.*

5.   THE BUSINESS PLAN   67
      *Elements and outline of a typical business plan. A sample business
      plan for a hypothetical image consultant.*

6.   SOME TRICKS OF THE TRADE   83
      *Suggestions for writing press releases. Using time effectively in
      wardrobe consulting. Wardrobe planning for men, including
      questionnaires. How to shop. Ten additional tips.*

7.   CORPORATE LOOKS FOR THE 21ST CENTURY   103
      *Update on corporate attire, including "business casual." Impact
      of the computer generation, global markets, and telecommuting.
      Women of color in the corporate environment.*

8.   REFINING YOUR IMAGE CONSULTING BUSINESS   127
     Taking stock, doing business seminars, expanding client services,
     surviving the down times, and other suggestions for established
     image consultants seeking to enhance their practices.

9.   PERSONALITY TYPES   139
     Learn about personality types and how this knowledge helps in
     image consulting. Includes sample tests for personality types.

10. RESOURCES   157
     Includes image consultant training programs, products, and
     associations.

INTRODUCTION

The idea for this book was inspired by June Davidson, president of the American Seminar Leaders Association. While I was attending a Professional Seminar Leaders workshop, June encouraged me to write a book about the image consulting industry. This made perfect sense to me—few people seem to understand what an image consultant actually does, and no books about the profession had yet been written.

Encouraged by June's energy and enthusiasm, I decided to draw on my 20-plus years of experience as a trainer and practicing image consultant to publish a book that would describe the industry and what it takes to be successful in it, review its history, and look at its future opportunities. Image consulting is a burgeoning industry, and in many ways is still in the process of establishing itself as a profession. I am confident, however, that it will be better understood and accepted, as industry standards are established and consultants are appropriately trained and certified.

This book will assist anyone considering image consulting as a full time or part time career. It also provides information and ideas for those already in the field. In addition, it can benefit anyone who is interested in fashion and style, and/or in presenting seminars.

So what is it that image consultants actually do? In brief, they advise and coach people on their appearance and presentation skills. Basic disciplines include clothing style, line, and color; grooming; speech and body language; etiquette; and much more, as you will discover in the pages to come.

Counsel from an image consultant gives a person knowledge and confidence—not unlike a "finishing school." When clients know they are presenting their best selves, there is no need to worry about appearance. They are freed up to focus their energy and attention on something other than themselves, whether it's listening to others or attending to the work at hand.

Image consultants also save clients money and time, and help them to simplify their lives. How? By assisting them in cleaning out their closets, by teaching them how to stretch their wardrobe budgets, and by ensuring that they will always have something appropriate to wear.

Image consultants provide services to groups as well as to individuals. They can assist corporate management in establishing dress codes and give seminars on how to achieve a polished, professional image. It is always easier for an outsider to come into the arena to address delicate issues such as attire, hygiene, and attitude. Image consultants provide seminars for association and business conferences as well as programs for community organizations. Often they volunteer their services in community endeavors, such as assisting battered women and advising women transitioning from welfare to work.

Who are likely image consultant candidates?

- People who like fashion and want to be engaged in a profession that encourages and helps others.

- Mothers who want to establish a home-based career that gives them time and scheduling flexibility.

- People as they near retirement, including baby boomers. Image consulting can be an exciting new career to pursue part time before retiring, and then either switch to full time or continue on a part time basis after retiring.

- Retired persons who want to continue working and stay in touch with the business community. Image consulting can provide an outlet for creativity as well as a mental challenge. Too much golf and bridge can get boring! Age is not a deterrent, since maturity is often associated with wisdom—especially if you have experience in related fields.

    As you, the reader, move forward on your journey, I wish you much success. I invite you to contact me.

                                        Brenda York-McDaniel

1 HISTORY OF THE IMAGE INDUSTRY

§ *The Father of Wardrobe Engineering*

It all began when Connecticut schoolteacher John T. Malloy became involved in a project researching the relationship between what teachers wore and how teenagers behaved in the classroom. What he discovered was that teachers' clothing had a significant impact on students' attitudes, attention span, and conduct.

Intrigued, Malloy continued his research, and in the early 1960's began supplementing his teacher's salary by advising lawyers, politicians, and ultimately large corporations on effective dress. In time, he was making enough money to change his profession "from teaching adolescents how to use language effectively to teaching adults how to use clothing effectively."

> *"A woman needs drive, ambition, intelligence, and education to move up the executive ladder. Without those qualities the best clothing in the world won't do anything for her. But even with them, if she doesn't have the right clothing, she won't get ahead."*
>
> John T. Malloy,
> *The Woman's Dress for Success Book*, 1977

In 1975, Malloy's best selling book on men's clothes, *Dress for Success,* was published, followed in 1977 by *The Woman's Dress for Success Book.* In both books Malloy emphasized that his advice was based not on personal opinion but on years of research; hence the term "wardrobe engineering." While aspects of image management for women had been around for a long time—e.g., wardrobe planning, modeling and finishing school courses—Malloy went a step further by addressing clothing requirements specifically for professional women who must compete with men for executive-level positions. He advocated a "business uniform" for women, consisting of a dark-colored, skirted suit—preferably medium gray or medium blue—worn with a contrasting color blouse, plain dark pumps, flesh-colored hose, and understated makeup.

Time marches on, and today Malloy's business uniform is considered outdated. However, his basic premise that certain industries require certain dress remains valid, as does his dictum that if you want to succeed, you have to look like you want to succeed. "My advice to women is based on the same principle as my advice to men," Malloy wrote. "Your clothes should move you up socially and in business, not hold you back."

§ A Pioneer Who Set a High Standard

While John Malloy was gathering material for his books, Emily Cho was contemplating leaving the corporate fashion world and striking out on her own. In 1970 she founded her own consulting firm, New Image, in New York City.

"When I first conceived of the idea of a consulting service, I knew that mine had to be different," Cho wrote in her 1978 book, *Looking Terrific*. "It was not going to be just a shopping service, but also a way of helping a woman with her <u>inner</u> as well as her <u>outer</u> qualities. Often clients come to me when they want to find or strengthen their own identities, beginning with their clothing image and working inward from there."

> *"Somewhere along the way, we women have acquired the idea that we should have an instinctive sense of style, that it ought to be born in us as an integral part of our femininity, and that, if it is lacking, we are somehow unwomanly."*
>
> Emily Cho,
> <u>Looking Terrific</u>, 1978

As one of the pioneers in image consulting, Cho set a high standard for the fledgling industry while she demonstrated to her clients that "clothing is not a bother and a bore but a terrific way to enjoy yourself and improve the quality of your life."

§ *From Individual to Corporate Clients*

Like Emily Cho, when I began my image consulting firm, York and Associates, in 1976, it was primarily to help individual clients develop workable wardrobes based on a capsule color scheme of four or five colors. I evaluated the person's wardrobe and suggested how to create new looks with existing pieces and accessories, while gradually building a new wardrobe. I advised on hairstyle and makeup and did personal shopping as well.

When the publication of Malloy's books created a demand to provide advice to businesses, I began doing more and more corporate seminars. I was hired by real estate firms, insurance companies, car dealerships, hotels, and retail stores to spruce up the image of their employees. Companies used this training to reward their employees or as a tactful way to tell them to shape up. It was good for employee morale, good for business, and financially lucrative for image consultants.

The 1980's   §   *The "Color-Me" Phenomenon*

At the Fashion Academy in Costa Mesa, California, in the 1970's, Gerry Pickney and Marge Swenson integrated a seasonal color theory into their curriculum. One of their students was Carole Jackson, who further refined the concept and wrote the book *Color Me Beautiful*. First published in 1980, it was a runaway best seller. Five years later the book had been reprinted 55 times!

The underlying theory to seasonal color analysis is that everyone's skin has either a blue or yellow undertone. Persons with a blue undertone to their skin should wear colors that also have a blue undertone, while those with a yellow undertone to their skin should wear colors with a yellow undertone. Within both groups there is further discrimination based on whether the colors worn should be clear or muted. Thus, the blue undertone group includes winter (clear colors) and summer (muted colors), and the yellow undertone group includes spring (clear colors) and autumn (muted colors).

Jackson explained all this in her book in a fun, easy-to-understand style, with plenty of color photographs to illustrate her point that the right colors enhance appearance while the wrong colors detract. Soon, women all over the country (and some men) were having their colors "done" and taking their color swatches to stores, where they looked for clothes in the right colors.

The fashion industry as a whole, however, ignored the seasonal color concept, frustrating consumers who could find nothing on the racks in their best colors. The silver lining in this situation was that the consumer could go to an image consultant who might advise her, for example, to buy a neutral dress or suit and then find a blouse or scarf that incorporated her most flattering color to wear near her face.

The consumer who bought the right color dress, but in a style that made her look and feel dumpy, could also be educated on the right line and style for her figure. An image consultant could also assist a client with shopping, or even do the shopping for the client. Time-strapped businesswomen (and men) were discovering that a good image consultant could save them time and money.

The "color-me" phenomenon also spawned multi-level companies that marketed cosmetics, lines of clothing, and even fragrances based on the seasonal concept. Some existing cosmetics companies were also motivated to categorize their makeup colors by warm and cool.

The downside in all this was that no standards existed for the image industry. Training for salespersons in the multi-level companies ranged from rigorous to nonexistent. Moreover, anyone could hang a shingle and call herself an image consultant. At the height of the color craze it seemed that just about every neighborhood had a self-proclaimed color consultant.

§ Promoting Professionalism in the Industry

By 1980 the market for corporate and individual image consultant services had grown to the point where I turned my attention to training other image consultants. I started the Academy of Fashion and Image to train prospective image consultants and to provide continuing education for experienced consultants.

As I continued to closely follow industry trends, I became increasingly alarmed at the growing number of untrained people entering the field, and thus detracting from the standing of legitimate consultants. As a result, in June of 1983 I founded the first industry association. The purpose of the

Association of Fashion and Image Consultants (AFIC) was to establish and enhance high standards of professionalism, competence, and achievement in the industry. During my four years as AFIC president the number grew from 25 to nearly 400 members in the U.S. and abroad.

> *"The industry's biggest problem is the people who call themselves image consultants and don't know what they're doing."*
>
> Brenda York, quoted in *The Washington Post*, May 17, 1983

In 1983, a small group of image consultants on the West Coast formed the Association of Image Consultants (AIC). In 1990 AFIC and AIC merged to form the Association of Image Consultants, International (AICI).

§ *Is Image Everything?*

The culture of the 1980s was a mixed blessing for image consultants. On one hand, business was booming. Individuals paid handsome sums for advice on how to look and dress, and were willing to buy expensive wardrobes. More and more corporations hired image consultants to conduct seminars on ways to project an image of success. By 1990 image consulting had become a $130 million a year industry.

In addition, image consulting was expanding beyond giving wardrobe and grooming advice. In the 1982-83 edition of the *Directory of Personal Image,* image services were divided into four categories: (1) dress and color, (2) speech/public appearance, (3) personal/public relations, and (4) motivation counseling.

However, there was a troubling aspect to the image business as well. Those of us who saw our role as helping clients put their best foot forward while remaining true to themselves sometimes felt outnumbered by those who bought into the emphasis on outward show and acting a part.

Malloy's Live for Success, published in 1981, placed primary importance on acting in order to advance in the corporate world. The author of *Dress for Success* fame frequently used actors in conducting research on executive attitudes and in training people to look and sound more upper-middle class, a prerequisite to attaining executive status, he claimed.

"There's no longer any question about the importance of image," commented political author Joe McGuinness in 1983. "It's reached the degree where you wonder where the image stops and the reality begins." It seemed particularly fitting for the times that the popular two-term U.S. president during the 1980's was a former professional actor.

The 1990's § *Hard Times and New Realities*

The affluence of the 1980's in the U.S. was tempered in the latter part of the decade by an economic downturn that continued until the mid-1990's.

Wave after wave of corporate restructuring resulted in layoffs that bit sharply into the ranks of middle and upper management, not just the lower echelon or new hires. In fact, those with seniority and high salaries were more likely to be targeted for dismissal because of the money it saved. Training and development budgets were slashed to the bone or eliminated entirely. As analysts warned that the days of job security were gone forever, employees at all levels feared losing their jobs, and caution and frugality became their watchwords.

There were other changes going on as well. New high-tech companies that were achieving phenomenal success were run by young entrepreneurs who didn't give a hoot about fashion and image, at least initially. Their laid-back style began to be echoed at more traditional companies in the adoption of dress down Fridays.

At the same time, the increasingly computerized business environment was allowing more people to avoid rush-hour traffic and telecommute from home. A number of women—tired of juggling the roles of hard-charging professional, devoted mother, and loving wife—were cutting back on work hours, starting their own home-based businesses, or leaving the work force altogether.

These were lean times for image consultants, except perhaps for those who had an established niche as media and communications advisors to politicians. Given the shifts in social and economic trends, attitudes, and priorities, we had to creatively rethink our profession.

§   *The Only Constant Is Change*

To be a successful image consultant requires staying abreast of trends, constantly ascertaining what needs of the population are not being met, and adapting services to meet those needs. Part of my job as a trainer is to facilitate the process of exploring ways in which image consultants can provide services that attract and benefit new clients.

In the early 1990's for example, I advised image consultants to target the needs of specific market segments, such as women of color and women over 50. I suggested obliging the public's bargain-hunting demands by becoming an expert personal shopper in discount and consignment shops as well as department and specialty stores. I recommended moving beyond color, makeup, and wardrobe to include personal development training—such as speech, body language, and skills marketing.

During the second half of the 1990's the economy picked up and grew more robust. Along with full employment and restored consumer confidence, the image consulting business rebounded, but with a softer, friendlier edge than that of the previous decade. Corporate dress was more relaxed except for the most conservative businesses; the uniform look was out. The cynicism of the 1980's yielded to an emphasis on inner beauty in conjunction with outward appearance.

In the mid-1990's the first wave of baby boomers turned 50, and seminars on maturing elegantly became popular. As a boomer myself, I can attest that today's fifty-plus women are not content to look like grandmother stereotypes!

In the late 1990's, image consultants were serving a wide-ranging clientele, from corporate lawyers focused on upward mobility to mothers moving off the welfare roles. People in the fiercely competitive high-tech sector turned to image consultants when they discovered that grooming mattered to potential customers after all. Companies again sought advice on visual image and improving customer relations.

As the century came to a close, corporations accounted for approximately one-third and individuals for two-thirds of the image industry's customer base. About half of these clients were men. Approximately 50 percent of image consultants were specializing in wardrobe planning and selection, while another 30 percent were offering training in speech and presentation skills.

§   *Outlook for the 21st Century*

The image consulting industry is poised for continued growth in the decades ahead. Contributing to this growth are the following scenarios in which the expertise of image consultants will be valuable in the 21st century:

- Economists and social scientists are predicting that there will be no such thing as a lifetime career in the 21st century. Instead, a person is

likely to have two, three, or more different
kinds of jobs during his lifetime.

- Americans will be working longer. The age at
  which people will be eligible for Social Security
  benefits is progressively being revised upward,
  so that when it's time for Generation X to
  retire, they will be in their 70's. Meanwhile, it
  is not likely that American culture will have
  changed its youth orientation, creating a
  formidable challenge for seniors.

- The world will keep getting smaller, making
  cross-cultural communications and proper
  etiquette more important than ever in business.

- Finally, more and more people will understand
  that image matters. It's just smart thinking for
  a person or a company to make the effort to
  create a favorable impression.

Although the outlook for image consulting in
the 2000's is good, it will always be subject to
economic ebbs and flows. It is not a static industry,
but a continually evolving one that must adjust to
public shifts in priorities, attitudes, and circum-
stances. Therefore, a successful image consultant in
the 21st century will constantly be on the alert for
new market segments to serve. (In the last part of
Chapter 2, practicing image consultants share their
ideas about what's ahead for the profession in the 21st
century.)

2 WHY CHOOSE IMAGE CONSULTING AS A CAREER?

An actress was complaining recently to a late night television host that it was so hard to find that "special someone." She had been dating a man who seemed like he could be the one until one evening she happened to glance down at his shoes. They were pointy-toed and weird looking. That did it; all romantic possibilities immediately evaporated, and she broke off the relationship. "I guess that was pretty shallow of me," she admitted, blushing. Then in the next breath she exclaimed, "But you should have seen those shoes! They were really awful!"

Shallow or not, in our image-conscious world we make judgments about other people all the time, based on nothing more substantial than a funky pair of shoes. This behavior occurs not only in romantic relationships, but in social and business situations as well.

Image consultants know this. Their job is to make their clients aware of the image "rules," and then teach them how to use the rules to benefit rather than hinder them. The image consultant's reward is not only financial remuneration but in the personal satisfaction derived from helping people improve their appearance and presentation skills and gain confidence in themselves.

How much does appearance matter? Consider that even

A BAD HAIR DAY CAN HURT YOUR SELF-ESTEEM, SAYS YALE RESEARCHER

According to a study by a Yale research team released in January 2000, "bad hair negatively influences self-esteem, brings out social insecurities, and causes people to concentrate on the negative aspects of themselves," *The Washington Post* reported.

The study, titled "The Psychological, Interpersonal, and Social Effects of Bad Hair," defined bad hair as hair that sticks out, needs cutting, is frizzy, damaged, poufy, fly-away, wild, badly cut, bushy, or greasy.

Marianne LaFrance, a psychology professor at Yale University, and a team of researchers conducted the study. Over a three-month period 120 Yale students were video-taped while recounting traumatic episodes with their hair. The study was financed by shampoo manufacturer Proctor & Gamble.

---

§ *Advantages of Image Consulting*

Image consulting is a growth industry offering unlimited opportunities, particularly for women. The profession has been featured in books such as *The Best Home Businesses for the 21st Century* by Paul & Sarah Edwards, and *101 Best Home-Based Businesses for Women* by Priscilla Huff, and in magazines such as *New Business Opportunities* and *Entrepreneur*. Advantages of a career in image consulting include the following:

- *Variety of Opportunities.* If you are interested in fashion and like helping people, image consulting offers many opportunities to do what you enjoy and express your creativity. There is a great variety of services you can offer, from individual consultations, to seminars in positive image training, to acting as an in-house consultant to corporations. The following are some of the areas in which image consultants advise clients:

- wardrobe analysis
  - color
  - line and style for figure type
  - wardrobe plan
  - closet analysis
  - personal shopping

- communications skills
  - speech and language
  - body language, posture, movement

- etiquette, protocol

- coaching for specific situations
  - job interviews
  - public appearances, television, radio

- modeling instruction

- hairstyle, grooming, makeup, fragrance

- diet, exercise

- fashion show production

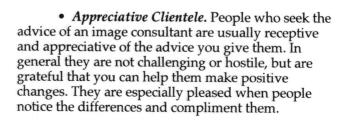

- *Appreciative Clientele.* People who seek the advice of an image consultant are usually receptive and appreciative of the advice you give them. In general they are not challenging or hostile, but are grateful that you can help them make positive changes. They are especially pleased when people notice the differences and compliment them.

- *Financially Rewarding.* It takes about two years to build a clientele large enough to support yourself. After three to five years it is not unrealistic to expect to gross $40,000 to $60,000 a year, depending on the opportunities in your area. Consultants whose business base is mainly corporations with deep pockets or who advise on niche topics, such as cross-cultural communications for international businesses, may earn $100,000 a year and up. Image advisors to high-level politicians may make $250,000 or more a year.

- *Flexible Hours.* You can pursue image consulting part time or full time; the choice is yours. Many start part time, eventually building a full time business. Because you can work from your home and choose your hours, this is an especially good profession for a parent. Furthermore, school holidays and summer vacations coincide with the times when there is less demand for your services.

- *Business Exposure for Children.* Having a home-based image consulting business allows time for you and your child during which you can explain your business as well as your goals and objectives. It provides many opportunities to teach your children about business and to set an example for them. They learn to respect your need for quiet when you are on the telephone. They hear you promoting your business, handling complaints, dealing with rejection. They see your reaction to success—such as when you get a good article in the press—and your disappointment when things don't go well. Small children can stay with you and work on their projects. Older children can help with mailings, computer input, and filing.

I asked my son, Peter Petro, Jr., who is now a young adult, to express what he learned from being around my business as he grew up. Here is what he wrote:

"At home I was often asked to answer the phone with a professional greeting rather than a simple 'Hello,' to close by thanking the caller, and to ask appropriate questions in between. Sometimes I would collate documents, stuff and label envelopes, and help with other projects like arranging press releases.

"These were not complicated tasks, but were small, repetitive ways of learning how to organize information and present it professionally, work under deadlines, follow directions, and take pride in a job well done as part of a 'grown-up' business. Without realizing it, I was learning to be responsible for important tasks.

"I was also afforded a lot of exposure to office communication between my mom's employees and contact with clients and the press. I was thus receiving practical training in how to communicate directives, how to present problems and questions, how to answer a question 'on my feet,' and how to express the total desired message: confident but considerate, professional but warm. I learned, through experience and osmosis, how to operate in a business environment."

• ***You Are Your Own Boss.*** As an entrepreneur you are investing in yourself and building for your future. No one is stepping on your creative toes. You make the plans and decisions concerning how to run the business and the direction in which you want it to go.

• ***Maturity Is a Plus.*** Image consulting can be a lifelong career, or one which you can enter after you have retired from another line of work. This is a profession in which you actually improve with age and experience. In fact, youth can limit your range of clients. People in their mid-thirties and upwards who aspire to executive-level jobs are not likely to seek advice on image from much younger consultants.

§ *Challenges*

• ***You Are Your Own Boss.*** One of the biggest attractions of image consulting also presents one of its biggest challenges. Being your own boss means that the buck stops with you. You and you alone are responsible for building a successful business. You must be able to make decisions, take risks, and accept the outcomes. In your everyday work routine you must be disciplined, organized, and have good time management skills.

• *No Steady Paycheck.* Image consulting work has peaks and valleys throughout the year, so you won't be earning a regular salary. You must work out a budget and stick to it, so that when business is good you put enough money away to get through the times when business is slow.

• *Subject to Economic Conditions.* Image consulting is very much subject to the ebbs and flows of the general economy. When the economy is good and businesses are thriving, individuals and companies are more open to the kinds of improvements suggested by image consultants, and they are more willing to pay for advice.

However, when the economy is unstable or in decline, individuals cut back on things they don't consider necessities and become avid bargain hunters. Corporations cut training programs and workers. Consulting with image specialists is generally considered a "frill" during economic hard times.

• *People Expect You to Look Perfect.* Because you are a walking, talking advertisement for your business, people expect your appearance to be perfect. Sometimes that can be a drag. You can't just run to the store in an old pair of sweats without makeup and hair out of place.

• ***Considerable Alone Time.*** Only a small fraction of image consulting work involves actually delivering services to clients. Much of the consultant's time is spent alone, planning, organizing and handling the business details. Since image consultants tend to be outgoing and people-oriented, it is vital to integrate connections with other people into a typical workweek. Have lunch with a friend. Call someone just to talk. Get together socially with others in the evening. In other words, balance the alone time with people interaction. Consider attending functions such as networking breakfasts, lunches, or "happy hours."

§   *Why They Chose Image Consulting— A Representative Sampling*

Most image consultants are women. The Academy of Fashion and Image (AFI) has trained women from all over the country and from all walks of life to be image consultants. The age range of AFI students is from the mid-twenties to the mid-sixties. What they have in common is an interest in fashion and a love of helping others. Also, most are entering the profession after having worked in one, two, three, or more different jobs. The following are profiles of some recent AFI students and their ambitions and objectives as image consultants.

• *From The Bronx, New York:* Image consulting is a brand new career for this nurse/nutritionist and human resources professional of 28 years. Her interest in fashion was sparked when she was a teenager and had to sew her own clothes to fit her 5'10", 150-pound frame. As a two-time breast cancer survivor, her goal is to work with the American Cancer Society's "Look Good - Feel Better" program.

- *From Lake Oswego, Oregon:* After living and working for seven years in Italy, this English teacher went into the business of relationship workshops for several years, then had a baby. The birth of her son kindled a desire to establish her own business, which compelled her to reflect on what she would really love to do. At one time she had done some modeling and liked the idea of facilitating others to improve their image and contribute to their total wellbeing.

- *From Jackson, Mississippi:* This beauty consultant and former model wants to integrate her psychology degree into her work. She chose image consulting because it provides an opportunity to help clients increase their self-esteem and self-confidence. She wants to assist people to become the best they can be in their personal and professional lives.

- *From Winthrop, Massachusetts:* Loan processor, legal assistant, flight attendant—this business administration graduate has had three different jobs in ten years. Now she sees image consulting as an opportunity to create, to help others look and feel fabulous, and to love what she does.

- *From Wichita, Kansas:* After graduating from college with a degree in music, this aspiring image consultant spent the next three years in the management end of the women's retail clothing business. She got a taste of what image consulting would be like when she coordinated outfits for

customers, joined other retailers in putting on a fashion show, and conducted a few workshops on how to dress for interviews. Her plan is to start out as a part time image consultant, eventually establishing her own full time business.

- *From Lubbock, Texas:* This ballet and Spanish dancer performed in Mexico, Puerto Rico, and Texas for several years, and then taught dance before retiring. She was selling cosmetics for a multi-level company when she decided to enroll at AFI to become a certified image consultant.

- *From Charlotte, North Carolina:* Fashion and image has been part of her life for over 15 years as a wholesaler of apparel and fashion accessories and as a cosmetics consultant. Now she plans to start her own home-based fashion and image consulting business part time, building to full time.

- *From Jonesboro, Georgia:* This former licensed practical nurse got her master's degree in social work after her children were grown, and spent 12 years as a supervisor in Atlanta's child welfare system until illness forced her to quit. Although she volunteers in homeless shelters, that is not enough to fulfill her desire to help others. She wants to apply her love of fashion design for large, tall women by advising clients at weight reduction clinics and by working with brides on limited incomes.

- *From Stevens, Pennsylvania:* After five years as a political staffer to a congressman and working as a political campaign coordinator, this young woman wants to establish a business advising politicians, sports figures, and other public figures on image.

  • *From Oshkosh, Wisconsin:* This trained psychologist says that for as long as she can remember she has had an interest in appearance, image, fashion, and the way they affect our perceptions of ourselves. She has her own consulting business providing training in cultural diversity and issues relating to women in the workplace. She plans to add image consulting to her repertoire of services.

  • *From Simpsonville, South Carolina:* Because this former fashion merchandiser is a petite woman, she has had to search for clothes that not only fit, but make her appear powerful instead of cute! When she realized that she wanted to stay in fashion but not continue her career as a buyer, she did some research and decided on image consulting. Her goal is to be self-employed and help people be their best.

§ Observations and Predictions about the Industry

Eleven professional image consultants from across North America responded to my invitation to share their opinions and predictions about the image industry. As you will see from their comments, image consultants do not necessarily think alike!

The most controversial issue concerns expanding services into other areas. Should image consultants stick to traditional markets involving image, or seek to incorporate other disciplines into their practices? Should there be limits as to how far afield image consultants should go? Does expanding the types of services offered enhance or dilute the credibility of the image industry?

Another topic of concern is the "business casual" trend of the 1990's. Are standards of dress going to deteriorate during the 21st century in the way that manners and etiquette did during the 1980's and 1990's? Will this result in more or less business for image consultants?

Several of the consultants spoke out on the need for improving professionalism in the industry—from implementing standards in training and certification, to paying better attention to their own appearance. They also mentioned that image consultants must take advantage of computer technologies in marketing and delivering services.

Upcoming markets cited include minorities, the aging population, busy professionals, and clients engaged in international businesses.

The following image professionals contributed their comments:

- **ROSALIND BISHOP** is an image consultant with the Divad Image Consulting Agency in Stockbridge, Georgia, and publishes a newsletter, *Divad Style.*

- **JACQUELYN (JAKI) BRITT** is an image consultant in Washington, D.C.

- **SUSAN FIGNAR** is a partner in the firm of Image Works Wonders, based in Itasca, Illinois. She is president of the Chicago chapter of the Association of Image Consultants, International (AICI).

- **LILLIAN JOHNSON,** whose image consulting business, Creative Elegance, is in New York City, is also a senior instructor at the Academy of Fashion and Image.

- **JOYCE KNUDSEN, Ph.D.,** trains image consultants in addition to providing consulting services through her company, The ImageMaker, Inc., in Franklin, Tennessee.

- **CYNTHIA LA SCHIAZZA** operates her firm, Image and More, in San Antonio, Texas.

- **SANDRA LANGHORNE** is an image consultant whose practice is in Winnipeg, Canada.

- **ELIZABETH MARCUM** is the founder of U by Design in Lake Oswego, Oregon.

- **PAT NEWQUIST** is the founder of Wardrobe Image in Tempe, Arizona. She is past president of the Phoenix chapter of AICI.

- **ALYCE PARSONS** is one of the founders of AIC and the author of four books. Her business, Universal Style & Associates, is in Monte Sereno, California.

- **JUDITH RASBAND** of the Conselle Institute of Image Management is based in Provo, Utah.

1. In your opinion, how can the image industry improve?

Rosalind Bishop: "Our industry must change with the times and technology. The presence of image consultants on the Internet is minimal. In order to remain competitive, our industry must claim a presence on the information super highway and implement innovative services."

Jaki Britt: "The image industry should hold those in the fashion industry accountable for the design and marketing of skimpy, trampy-looking clothing. Some of the work produced as 'fashion' is a disgrace!"

Susan Fignar: "We need to raise the bar regarding training and certification. The image industry is confusing: Some individuals have attended a 'formal' training program while many have not. There are many different areas of specialization for example, makeup and skin care, wardrobe, etiquette, protocol, corporate communications, etc. Some individuals started their businesses because they like to shop. Yet we all refer to ourselves as image consultants. I feel strongly that all image consultants need to be knowledgeable about the trends and issues in the workplace regarding dress, grooming, etiquette, demeanor, and attitude.

"In addition, I suggest that advanced levels of training and development be made available to seasoned consultants (seven-plus years of experience) and that the consultants give back/share what they have learned by mentoring new consultants."

- continued -

How the image industry can improve, continued

Joyce Knudsen: "The industry can improve by communicating with the public and educating people about the importance of self-esteem and personal development. Wellness also should be part of this scenario."

Sandra Langhorne: "As business becomes more global, the image industry should be prepared to explain the etiquette principles of diverse cultures."

Cynthia La Schiazza: "There should be more mentoring for aspiring and new image consultants. Also, we should be providing the public with more education about what we can do for them."

Elizabeth Marcum: "The public's perception of the industry would be improved if there were universal standards for certification of image consultants."

Pat Newquist: "What stands out most to me is the lack of professional dress of image consultants. We must look the part! Also, we need to work much smarter. Computer skills and the ability to use the Internet are a must."

Alyce Parsons: "We need statistics from image consultants so that we have a better idea of how our industry is doing and how many people we are helping."

Judith Rasband: "Image consultants must steer clear of fringe, flimsy, and fad topics or trends, such as iridiology, seasons, feng shui, and so on. We must stick with a solid art and science base of information on which to build our business for the long term."

2. What are your predictions for the image industry? How do you see it changing over the next 20 years?

Rosalind Bishop: "With persistence, professional training, and flexibility, the image industry will be perceived as having a critical influence on professional success. Also, the industry will expand into other areas."

Susan Fignar: "Corporate image consultants/trainers will form strategic alliances with trainers in complementary areas. For example, our company has a strategic alliance network on our website that gives our clients one-stop shopping for services that we do not offer, but a member of our network does. There are referral fees, so the relationships are mutually beneficial."

Joyce Knudsen: "There will be more long-distance consulting. With the accessibility of the Internet, image consultants will consult online, offer courses, send CDs, and e-mail clients all over the world. Already 60 percent of colleges offer distance learning programs. If you can get a college degree without leaving your home, why not an image degree?"

Elizabeth Marcum: "The image industry has enormous growth potential. Some consultants may become more specialized; concentrating, for example, on wardrobe and personal shopping or speech and body language. Corporate seminars will become even more popular. I foresee a return to manners, with etiquette lessons in demand. I also see image

- continued -

Predictions, continued

consultants becoming information managers, sponsoring seminars and workshops, and directing clients to professionals with expertise in a variety of image-related fields."

Sandra Langhorne: "Training in Internet and technology etiquette will grow. There will be more schools providing image consultant training, and more students will receive certification so that the industry as a whole will gain greater respect and recognition."

Pat Newquist: "One area I see taking off is video conferencing with clients around the globe. If we have a computer and video camera, the world is our client."

Alyce Parsons: "I predict the industry will enlarge and incorporate other systems, such as enneagrams and feng shui. Image consultants who do branch out will need to be certified in these disciplines."

Judith Rasband: "Many fashion retailers are banking on consumer demand for casual, very casual, and super casual which translates to sporty, sexy, and just plain sloppy. The teen to thirty-somethings place no value on clothing versatility, creativity, or visual individuality. We are losing our fashion options, particularly men, as more and more retailers drop their nicer clothing lines and menswear clothiers go out of business."

What products are needed?

Jaki Britt: "Clothing made from natural fabrics in styles that allow for comfort, wear, movement, and longevity."

Susan Fignar: "Better quality training products along with the resources for Power Point-type presentations, unique visuals, online learning, and affordable customized products."

Lillian Johnson: "Professional image visuals for minorities, or visuals that include more minorities, such as a training video on color analysis. It is sometimes difficult to use materials that do not reflect the minority audience.

"We also need more materials to address the needs of the plus-size figure. The average dress size in America is 14, and yet there are only a few image consultants specializing in the market for larger women. Besides the challenges of finding and wearing the right clothes and colors, these women often have self-esteem and health-related problems. In addition, we need more books, videos, and other materials focusing on the maturing woman."

Joyce Knudsen: "We have many books about image, but what we need are workbooks that people can use as they go along. An image journal comes to mind, with step-by-step instructions on how to work toward a 'more wonderful you.'"

Sandra Langhorne: "Updated videos for classroom learning, and books and magazines that focus on the industry. "

- continued -

Products needed, continued

Elizabeth Marcum: "Cosmetics kits geared to seasonal palettes specifically for image consultants to use with clients, and clothing lines that consultants could market with their services."

Pat Newquist: "Our current clients wish we had the capability to put everything on computer CDs. I think there will be a growing demand for software programs to do that."

Alyce Parsons: "Travel packing as we become more international."

Judith Rasband: "Accurate, practical, powerful educational materials. But more importantly, economical and effective ways of getting these materials into the mainstream."

What are some upcoming markets?

Rosalind Bishop: "Home-based and small businesses are markets for image consultants willing to expand their services to provide assistance and advice in how to start, manage, and grow their businesses as well as enhance their business image."

Jaki Britt: "Stay-at-home workers, whether self-employed or telecommuting."

Susan Fignar: "(1) Young professionals between 23 and 33 years old, especially those in the technology field.

- continued -

Upcoming markets, continued

"(2) Individuals who are going through job/career searches due to downsizing. We were shocked to discover that many individuals had eight to 20 years at the company laying them off and didn't have a clue as to how to market/sell themselves.

"(3) Retailers. There is so much competition out there because of business casual dress, outlets, and the never-ending 'special sales.' Retail clothiers would benefit tremendously by training their employees in how to build good, lasting relationships with customers.

"In addition, certain trends in society—the business casual craze, casual dining habits, and endless hours watching television and surfing the net—have resulted in poor people skills, casual demeanor, lack of awareness of etiquette, sloppy appearance, and so forth. As these trends continue to grow so will the need for image consultants to educate individuals and corporations on business and social etiquette, civility, appearance, demeanor, attitude, team building, how to build successful client/personal relationships, networking, and personal marketing."

Lillian Johnson: "Ethnic clients, such as African Americans, Hispanics, and Asians. Also, plus-size women and maturing women."

Cynthia La Schiazza: "Minorities, the physically challenged, those reentering the work force, telecommuters, and small business owners."

- continued -

Upcoming markets, continued

Sandra Langhorne: "Technology etiquette, cross-cultural etiquette, professional image training in non-traditional industries, and consultations with and seminars for mature audiences."

Elizabeth Marcum: "The aging population will be looking for specialty skin care and anti-aging nutritional products. I also detect a growing interest in holistic skin care and cosmetics, including Ayurvedic skin and beauty treatments.

"In addition, among busy professionals there is an increasing need for organizational consultants who can bring order to both office and home environments. I foresee many professionals hiring 'lifestyle coordinators' who do everything from wardrobe planning to interior design."

Alyce Parsons: "Baby boomers and senior citizens will continue to be sizable market segments."

Judith Rasband: "Unless the casual trend is countered or reversed, there will be no upcoming markets or a 'fashion' industry as we have known it. Teens will wear t-shirts and jeans, the fit and firm will wear tunics and leggings, and the elderly will be in sweats."

Notes

3 WHAT IT TAKES TO BE AN IMAGE CONSULTANT

§ *Snapshot of Susan*

Susan Smith can't remember a time when she wasn't interested in fashion. As a little girl she would spend hours designing outfits for her paper dolls. She loved Cinderella stories in which the ugly duckling teenager turned into a swan simply by changing her hairstyle, applying makeup, and slipping into a stunning outfit.

In high school Susan was the one whose friends asked her to go clothes shopping with them. During her first year in college she quickly learned where to shop for the best bargains in clothes, and was voted best dressed in her dormitory two years in a row. Later, in her job as a speech therapist, Susan received numerous compliments on her tasteful, low-key style of dress. When special occasions came up, Susan's coworkers solicited her advice on what to wear.

Susan met her husband at an amateur theater group, one of many community activities in which she was involved. Warm, friendly, and outgoing, Susan was often approached to be on committees. Never one to avoid the spotlight, she liked to take charge and particularly enjoyed giving talks—having an audience energized her.

After ten years as a speech therapist, Susan was ready for a change. She wanted to try something new and different, something compatible with her desire to be of service while allowing her to spend more time at home with her two children. One Saturday afternoon, while waiting in a long checkout line at the grocery store, Susan began to do something she often did to pass the time. In her mind's eye she changed the beige sweater on the man to her left to a more flattering medium gray shade. She gave the lady in front of her a pants suit with more flattering lines and an up-to-date hairstyle. "Wouldn't it be fun to do this for a living?" she thought.

Several weeks later, Susan went to the library and checked out a book on home-based businesses by Paul and Sarah Edwards. One of the listings was "Image Consultant." Susan could barely contain her excitement as she read the business description and realized that this was exactly what she was looking for! But to quit her current job to start her own business would mean losing a steady paycheck and financial sacrifices by the family. She talked it over with her husband and he agreed to be the breadwinner for the time that it took for Susan to get herself established as an image consultant. They worked out a budget that cut out many of the luxuries to which they were accustomed. To contribute at least some income, Susan started a private practice in speech therapy, taking on a limited number of clients.

Susan investigated training programs for certification as an image consultant, enrolling in the program that appeared to be right for her. She completed her training, and because of the contacts

she had already established in the community, had no
difficulty getting her image consultant business off
the ground. Her first client was an acquaintance from
the PTA who was running for political office. When
Susan volunteered to coordinate and narrate a fashion
show for a charity benefit, she was given a write-up in
the local newspaper that resulted in several clients.
She put together wardrobes for the mayor's wife, a
young trial lawyer, and a recently promoted
corporate executive. She provided fashion tips on a
local television show and persuaded the local
community college to include her in a segment of a
business course.

Within a few years, Susan had a thriving
business that was continuing to grow through the
referrals of satisfied clients. It was a dream come
true; Susan was doing something she truly loved and
was getting paid for it.

§ *Characteristics of a Successful Image Consultant*

Susan Smith is a fictional character, a composite of the students I've trained over the years to
become image consultants. Although each student is
unique, I have discovered that those who go on to
establish successful businesses tend to share certain
interests, talents, and personality traits.

• *Service Oriented.* A good image consultant
cares about her clients. She loves her job because of
the pleasure and satisfaction she gets from helping a

client look his or her best. She sees image enhancement as self-improvement, not projection of a phony
image. She believes she is offering a valuable service
and feels a special pride when a client radiates new
confidence from the inside out.

• *Extroverted.* Successful image consultants
are usually extroverts. They are energized through
their interaction with people. Like the best
salespersons, they are warm and enthusiastic, with an
easy-going manner and a sense of humor. They are
joiners of community and business organizations.
Often they are leaders and natural-born performers.
They enjoy giving talks, holding workshops,
appearing on television, and attending conventions
and trade shows.

Introverted types are less people-oriented and
therefore not as likely to gravitate toward the
profession. They may have an exquisite fashion sense
and some great marketing ideas, but making public
appearances and selling themselves and their services
drains them of energy. If an introvert has a burning
desire to go into the business, it is recommended that
she partner with an extrovert who relishes the public
contact, doesn't mind making the cold calls, and
appreciates the different kind of skills her shy
colleague brings to the business.

• *Poised and Confident.* Poised, articulate,
tactful, and well-mannered, the successful image
consultant carries herself with confidence. Her
appearance is polished and professional and her
grooming impeccable. She has a creative flair and a
sense of her own personal style. She keeps up with

current fashion and has a knack for adapting trends in ways that accommodate and harmonize with the personalities and physical characteristics of her clients.

Rate Yourself

For each set of characteristics, 5 corresponds most strongly with the characteristic listed on the left and 1 corresponds most strongly to its polar opposite on the right. 5 is the minimum and 25 the maximum total points for the five sets.

Extroverted	5 4 3 2 1	Introverted
Fashion-Wise	5 4 3 2 1	Not Much Style Sense
Poised and Confident	5 4 3 2 1	Unsure of Self/Lacking Social Skills
Sensitive/Intuitive	5 4 3 2 1	Inattentive/Oblivious
Disciplined	5 4 3 2 1	Poor Time Management/ Disorganized

The higher the score, the more of a natural you are for image consulting. The lower the score, the harder you will have to work to succeed.

• *Sensitive and Intuitive.* Important traits for an image consultant include being observant, intuitive, and a quick study. She must size up her client's needs, strengths, and personality quickly and accurately, reading between the lines as necessary. She is a good listener and treats her clients with

respect and tact. She communicates successfully by
tailoring her approach to suit the individual client.

• *Disciplined.* The advantages of image
consulting--such as being your own boss and having
a flexible schedule--can be the undoing of the person
who tends to put things off or has a lackadaisical
attitude. A business-like approach, with the ability to
structure time wisely, is essential to a successful
business.

§ Background & Education

It is advantageous but not necessary for an
image consultant to have a college degree. Some
college education is helpful, particularly in the liberal
arts, since many potential clients will be college
educated. Desirable experience includes fashion-
related fields such as clothing design and/or sales,
cosmetics, or modeling; teaching, speech, psychology,
public relations, acting, or broadcasting; marketing,
accounting, or business management; or some
combination of the above elements as you probably
will be drawing on most, if not all, of them.

§ Training

I can't stress enough the importance of
appropriate training if you really want to be a
successful image consultant. Without it, you
shortchange your clients, damage your credibility,
and hurt the image of the profession. Investigate the
training program you are considering. Remember,

you <u>want</u> the training to be rigorous because you want to be prepared to do your job right.

QUESTIONS TO ASK
ABOUT A PROSPECTIVE TRAINING PROGRAM

1. Is certification as an image consultant offered? What is involved in getting a certificate?

2. What does the course work include? How long does the program take to complete? Can you send me a syllabus?

3. Beyond the basics, if there is specialized expertise I need that you don't offer, can you provide me with the names of programs and/or people who do?

4. Do you offer a mentoring program?

5. Can you provide me with at least three references from students who completed the course, including their telephone numbers?

- ***Training Program Recommendations.*** If you plan to run your own image consulting business, and if you expect to work with individual clients and groups, the training program you select should offer the following <u>as a minimum</u>:

  - Color, fabric, line, and style of clothing for both women and men
  - Wardrobe planning
  - Business plans
  - Public relations and marketing
  - Conducting seminars

- Referrals for specialized training
- Mentoring and networking opportunities

Ideally, information about body language, speech, social etiquette, and corporate protocol would be incorporated into the course work or offered as separate courses. It is also desirable that the training institution offer continuing education for established consultants.

AFI graduate Jennifer Johnson writes:

I found through extensive Internet research that while many companies offer certification, there are different ways of achieving that certificate. Most programs require selling or purchasing of products, especially cosmetics.

It is important to know before you sign up for the program that you are truly interested in image consulting. I say this because that will allow you to grow in the direction you need to develop and enhance your company.

Factors to consider:

1. instructor, program, mentor support
2. availability of support
3. reputation of the program
4. references from past students and clients
5. your primary goals in achieving certification, and how each program can meet those goals

§ *Other Factors*

• *Be Financially Prepared.* Building a successful image consulting business takes time. Meanwhile, you have living expenses to meet. Note that our fictional heroine, Susan Smith, approached her decision to become an image consultant realistically by confronting the financial situation up front. She and her husband discussed it and worked out a budget. He understood that when Susan quit her full time job as a speech therapist he would have to carry the financial load. She agreed to supplement his income by seeing a limited number of speech therapy clients in private practice.

Everyone has a different financial scenario to consider. Clearly, those in the best position are the ones who have partners willing to bear the financial burden for awhile or who have other sources of capital. Full time homemakers and others who have not been revenue producers won't have to make as many financial adjustments as those who lose their sole source of income when they give up their salaries to pursue image consulting. Those without another source of financial support may decide to take the image training and do image consulting part time while keeping their full time jobs until they are more financially secure.

• *Have Supportive Relationships.* Image consulting is a demanding profession, not a hobby or frivolous pastime. Sometimes people don't take seriously the professional who works from home, particularly at the beginning. They assume she doesn't have the same time constraints that would exist if she were employed in an outside business. It is very important to respect the image consultant's work and support her by upholding the boundaries and limits she sets.

§ *My Story*

In the mid-1970's I was inspired by the books of John T. Malloy and Emily Cho to hang out my own shingle as a fashion and image consultant. Because of my background and interests, this was not a big leap. My previous experience included fashion and cosmetics merchandising, curriculum development, and training, and I served as head instructor at a modeling school. In addition, as a newly-single mother of a nine-month-old son, I liked the idea of running a business out of my home and having flexible hours.

My first client was a person who belonged to one of the same social organizations I did. She recommended me to another individual, and it wasn't very long before I had a number of clients, all through personal referrals. One of these referrals was a real estate broker who invited me to give a seminar at a sales meeting. This led to seminars for other real estate companies, for the Board of Realtors, and at real estate conventions. In addition, I was asked to write articles for real estate trade publications.

Seminars for car dealerships followed, then hotels, insurance companies, professional associations, government agencies, and a women's clothing store. Often people would tell me that they wanted to do what I was doing. It occurred to me that I could train them, and so in 1983 I founded the Academy of Fashion & Image for aspiring image consultants. I also taught classes at a local "open" university on how to start one's own business. For a time I moved my business completely out of my home, renting classroom space for training and a separate space for a business office.

While I was building my business, I was being sought by the media as an expert in the image consulting industry. I was quoted in many periodicals, including major daily newspapers, such as *The Washington Post, Chicago Tribune, New York Daily News,* and *USA Today;* popular magazines, such as *Newsweek, People, U.S. News & World Report, Glamour* and *Mademoiselle;* and various business publications, such as *Wall Street Journal, Changing Times, Success,* and *Entrepreneur.* This publicity further enhanced my reputation and helped attract more clients.

In summary, I was able to start and successfully build an image consulting business because I had the background, interest, and commitment required for the job. I knew what I wanted to do and was not afraid to jump in and do it. If you, too, have the desire, drive, and initiative to become an image consultant, you will find that it can be a career that is both personally and financially rewarding.

Notes

GETTING STARTED

§ Full Time or Part Time?

Finances often drive the decision to start out as either a part time or full time image consultant. It usually takes a couple of years to establish a full time image consulting business. Consequently, the new consultant may opt to keep her day job while counseling clients during evening and weekend hours. Many employed individuals prefer after-hours consultations anyway.

§ Start-Up Capital

Part time or full time consultants can expect to spend in the range of $5,000 to $20,000 (including the cost of training) for start-up costs; less if you already have some of the equipment, furniture, and clothing; more if you want to establish an office outside the home and/or purchase new, top-of-the-line equipment, furniture, and a designer-label wardrobe.

<u>Major Business Items</u>

Training program leading to certification

Supplies   • business cards
                  • letterhead stationery
                  • office supplies

	• color drapes or swatches • demo cosmetics
Equipment	• telephone • voice mail, answering machine, or message service • computer • printer • fax/copier
Furniture	• desk, chair, and lamp • filing cabinet • mirror(s)
Wardrobe (*minimum*)	• two or three seasonally appropriate outfits, including accessories, shoes, handbag(s) and/or briefcase, coat
Other	• business license • reference books, magazines and other periodicals • handouts and visual aids
Nice to have	• small conference table • brochure describing your business, services offered, credentials • tape recorder • instant print camera and/or photographer services • camcorder and/or video services • digital camera

- scanner to use with computer

Consultant
services
- accountant
- graphics designer for professional logo, brochure, handouts
- printer
- photographer
- videographer
- editorial services
- computer services
- clerical assistance

§ *The Business Side*

- ***Name.*** Decide on the name of your business. The name can be non-specific (e.g., Susan Smith & Associates) or related to image consulting (e.g., Better Image, LLC). Whatever name you choose, keep it businesslike and avoid anything ambiguous or cute.

- ***Accountant.*** Ask around for the name of a good accountant. He/she will be the most important outside consultant you'll have, particularly in regard to paying consultants, tax deductions, general tax advice, and recommended bookkeeping systems. His/her first order of business will be to advise you as to what legal entity your business should operate under, such as sole proprietorship or limited liability corporation.

- ***Bank Account.*** Open a separate account for your business.

- **Business License.** Many jurisdictions require an in-home business to have a business license. Inquire at your county courthouse. Fees are based on anticipated annual income generated by the business.

- **Insurance.** Your homeowner's or renter's insurance policy may need to be increased to cover your home office. Also, you may need additional liability insurance if you plan to deliver services to clients in your home.

§ Delivering Services: Your House or Theirs?

Image consultants often go to the client's home or office to provide services. If you plan to do so, ask if a full-length mirror is available. If not, there are inexpensive, lightweight, full-length mirrors available that you can tote with you. Before purchasing, make sure it fits in your car. Also, take a makeup mirror and a natural-light lamp with you.

If you plan to counsel some individual clients in your home, you must provide an attractive, comfortable, space. If you will be using your living and dining rooms, it goes without saying that they must be neat—no children's toys on the floor, dog hairs on the sofa, or papers lying around. The bathroom must be clean. If the full-length mirror is in the bedroom, then that room also must be tidy. Adequate, natural lighting is another requirement. You may need to invest in a lamp with special bulbs that mimic natural light, as well as a makeup mirror with good lighting.

It is best to offer color analysis in a group setting. If you have just one client, consider asking two or three friends of yours to join the session (for free). Figure out ahead of time how you will set up the lighting and seat the group.

§   *Identifying Potential Clients*

Most image consultants start with individual clients, such as:

- job seekers
- professionals in businesses that deal with the public
- executives and other employees aspiring to move up the corporate ladder
- home-based entrepreneurs and consultants
- politicians and local dignitaries
- television personalities and news anchors
- anyone in the public eye

Social, professional, educational, and various community groups can offer opportunities to present workshops/seminars and can also be a source for individual clients. Examples include:

- groups that cater to singles
- senior citizen groups
- community organizations seeking ways to raise funds
- adult education centers

- open universities, community/recreation centers

Slightly more than a third of those in the image field move into corporate consulting. This area of the business includes seminars at industry conventions and trade shows as well as workshops for individual companies that sell to or otherwise deal with the public, such as:

- hotels
- insurance companies
- law firms
- financial services providers
- public relations firms
- hospitals and other medical services providers, including rehabilitation centers
- merchandisers of various products, including cars, electronics, and clothing

In addition to businesses and their respective associations, other potential clients include:

- government agencies
- social service organizations
- employment centers
- retirement homes
- educational institutions

§   Steps in Developing a Clientele

- ***Consider Providing Some Services for Free.*** In the beginning, consider offering your services free of charge to a community group. The publicity and good will that are generated can help your business get off the ground. Be sure to send press releases to your local newspapers before and after the event. Include one or two photographs of yourself, perhaps a head shot and an action photo related to what you will be doing for the event. Try to piggyback one event with another, such as in the following examples:

Offer to produce a fashion show as a benefit for a community group or cause. Ask a local store to provide the clothes and the models for the show, or use models from the community group.

If the collaboration with the store is successful, join forces again to get on a local television show. Come up with a theme that ties in fashion trends for the coming season with a socially relevant topic, such as clothes for mature women returning to the job market, or for recent college graduates entering the work force for the first time. Send the producer of the show a one-page proposal that clearly states what you are offering and provide examples of the kinds of tips you will give on the air.

Offer to give seminars at a local college for graduating seniors. Prepare a one-page proposal for the guidance department or dean of a specific school at the college. Tailor the seminar to specific groups -- graduates in computer technology or business administration, for example. Include tips on dressing and presenting oneself for the job interview and on the job. Have a photographer take some pictures during the seminar. If the seminars go well, offer to

do them again the following year, but this time for a fee.

    <u>Write a feature article</u> for a local newspaper, covering the same topic as the college seminar. Include photographs. Incorporate what you learned from the college seminar into a course that you propose to teach for a fee in an open university setting or adult education center.

    • *Keep Abreast of Current Events.* Read newspapers and news magazines regularly to get ideas for potential clients. Trends in popular culture provide springboards for ideas to generate business. If you want to conduct corporate seminars, study the business sections. What industries are doing well? Businesses that are flourishing are more open to proposals for training than those that are struggling. What companies are merging and downsizing? They may be open to your expertise in helping laid off employees prepare for job interviews elsewhere. Are there businesses with specific image problems that you could help solve with employee training or public relations events?

    • *Cultivate Specific Market Segments.* Once you've gotten your foot in the door of one type of business, market your services to other companies in the same field. For example, if you give a seminar to employees at a hotel, add this experience to your resume and use it as part of your sales pitch to subsequent hotels and associations that deal with elements of the hotel business. The same principle applies to your individual clientele. For example, after you've advised a graduating college student about how to present himself on a job interview, you may want to consider making this your specialty, counseling not only individual college graduates but pitching your services to private and public employment agencies. Working with individuals can lead to workshops for organizations, just as delivering seminars for organizations can result in business from individual clients.

§ *Network, but Maintain a Balance*

At least half your time will be spent marketing your services as opposed to delivering them, so always be on the alert for ways to attract new clients. Nearly everybody has situations in which they want to look their best, so nearly everybody you meet is a potential client. Because you never know where a referral will come from, let people know about your new business. Carry your business cards at all times. Become active in community organizations. Join business and professional organizations, including your local chamber of commerce.

I recommend attending at least three meetings of any association before joining to decide if it will benefit you. Determine the cost per year with dues, monthly meetings, and child care. Is it worth it? What will you gain? Are there potential clients in this organization? What will you learn?

Networking is important, but don't carry it too far. It can be tiring to always be in the selling mode, not to mention off-putting to your family and friends. Personally, I never market my services to relatives, friends, members of my church, or other social groups if I don't feel right about it. You may want to limit your networking to business situations. At any rate, you need to identify what boundaries you are comfortable with. Your aim should be to achieve a balance between what is good for your business and still have a separate, rewarding, personal life.

§ *Advertising Versus Publicity*

Image consulting is a profession that depends largely on word of mouth and referrals to attract clients. Traditional advertising is not particularly effective. Satisfied customers, your own personal appearance and demeanor, and media publicity are your best advertisements. Write press releases and feature articles for local newspapers. (See Chapter 6 for ideas on writing a press release.) Familiarize yourself with local radio and television shows and come up with ideas to appear on them. Sometimes this will involve a collaborative effort with other individuals and groups in your community.

If you decide to advertise, follow these budget-wise suggestions:

- Avoid display ads in newspapers and magazines. They are expensive and not particularly effective.

- Spend your time and money on editorial-type ads. These are ads that are written like news or feature stories.

- Test a classified ad in a newspaper. They are inexpensive and should be run at least three consecutive times.

- List your business in directories.

- Develop fliers and brochures describing your business.

- Participate in fund raisers. Provide your services as door prizes.

§ *What to Charge*

Fees charged by image consultants in the U.S. vary, depending on the region of the country, the demand for services, the types of services offered, and the experience of the consultant. In general, the range is $45 to $125 an hour for counseling individual clients on visual image (including wardrobe), although some high-end consultants charge as much as $250 an hour. (I recommend a two-hour minimum.) If the consultant offers package deals to individuals, the hourly rate may work out to be less. Some consultants charge higher rates for speech and language coaching, as much as $75 to $300 an hour.

Charges for corporate seminars are higher and are contingent on a number of factors, including length of the seminar, topics covered, number of participants, quality of handouts, and the financial resources of the company. A rate of $1,000 to $3,000 a day is not out of line and can go higher, depending on what the market will bear.

Better Image, LLC
1234 FIRST STREET
RIVERTON, OHIO 54321

LIST OF CONSULTANT SERVICES FOR
INDIVIDUAL CLIENTS

Hourly Fee: $75

PACKAGES

1.   **Basic: $150**
     - Color Analysis - *What colors flatter you; what colors to avoid.*
     - Figure Analysis and Clothing Line & Style - *What styles suit your figure.*

2.   **Personal Wardrobe Plan: $400**
     - Color Analysis
     - Figure Analysis and Clothing Line & Style
     - Closet Analysis - *Assessment of what works and what doesn't in your current wardrobe.*
     - Wardrobe Plan - *Individualized plan for updating your current wardrobe.*

3.   **Wardrobe Plan & Shopping: $450**
     - Color Analysis
     - Figure Analysis and Clothing Line & Style
     - Closet Analysis
     - Wardrobe Plan
     - Shopping with Client

Additional Services at Hourly Rates Include:
- Personal Coaching: Speech, Body Language, and Presentation Skills
- Social Etiquette & Business Protocol

Referrals to Hair Stylist and Makeup Artist Available

Susan Smith
012-345-6789

Better Image, LLC
1234 FIRST STREET
RIVERTON, OHIO 54321

CORPORATE SEMINARS

Suggested Topics:

- POLISHING YOUR PROFESSIONAL IMAGE - Includes how to create a positive first impression, body language, voice, verbal communication, and wardrobe.

- CORPORATE PROTOCOL - Includes introductions, proper handshake, dining skills, telephone etiquette, international business protocol.

- JOB INTERVIEW SKILLS

- PRESENTATION SKILLS

     ---- **AND MUCH MORE. Call to discuss designing a seminar to fit your needs.**

Fees (plus expenses):

Full Day Seminar: (six hours plus one hour lunch break)	$1,500
Half Day (three hours) Seminar:	$1,000
Two Hour Seminar:	$ 800
One Hour (or less) Seminar:	$ 500
Planning & Observing on Location (two hours):	$ 85

     - Client to reproduce handouts from masters provided.

Terms: 50% of fee at booking. Balance on day of seminar.

Susan Smith, 012-345-6789

§ Ancillary Businesses

If your image consulting business is slow to get off the ground, you might want to consider supplementing your income by offering services through established businesses, such as being a personal shopper for a retail clothing store or offering makeup tips, color analysis, and other services by appointment through a beauty salon. Other options include selling makeup or accessories, or holding home-based trunk shows of made-to-order clothing three or four times a year.

§ Suggested Beginning Reference Library

• Cho, Emily, and Fisher, Neila. *Instant Style: 500 Professional Tips on Fashion, Beauty, and Attitude.* HarperCollins, 1996. ISBN 0-06-273399-0.

• Davidson, Jeffrey, and Sanow, Arnold. *You Can Start Your Own Business.* Washington Publications, Inc., 1991. ISBN 0-925052-02-7.

• Edwards, Paul and Sarah. *Getting Business to Come to You.* Tarcher/Putnam, 2nd edition, 1998. ISBN 0-87477-845-X. Also, *Making It on Your Own.* G.P. Putnam's Sons, 1991. ISBN 0-87477-636-8.

• Falke, Martha. *The First Four Seconds: Things Successful Men Know about Dressing for Power.* Falcon House Publishing, 1990. ISBN 0-9627227-0-7.

• Goldsmith, Olivia, and Collins, Amy. *How to Find Your Personal Style and Look Fantastic Every Day!* HarperCollins-Wakefield Group, 1995. ISBN 0-06-109394-7.

• Griessman, B. Eugene. *Time Tactics of Very Successful People.* McGraw-Hill, 1994. ISBN 0-07-024644-0.

• Nix-Rice, Nancy. *Looking Good.* Palmer/Pletsch Publications, 1998. ISBN 0-935278-42-7.

• Petticord, Jo. *Look Like a Winner after 50 with Care, Color & Style.* The National Writers Press, 3rd edition, 1997. ISBN 0-88100-082-5.

• Klensch, Elsa. *Style.* The Berkley Publishing Group, 1995. ISBN 0-399-521.52-5.

§   *Real-Life Success Stories*

One of the joys of my job as a trainer is the opportunity to meet the wonderful people who are attracted to the Academy of Fashion & Image. There may be some in this industry who are more geared to the superficial aspects of image consulting, but fortunately, AFI students do not fit that mold. When their training is finished, AFI graduates usually keep in touch, and I love to follow their success. I would like to introduce you to three AFI graduates whom I consider role models for new image consultants. They knew what they wanted to do, and immediately after they completed their training, wasted no time in getting started.

• **JILL AUSTIN** had a BS degree in fashion merchandising and 15 years of experience in retail buying, sales, and management when she came to AFI for training as an image consultant. As soon as she returned to Bowling Green, Kentucky, she began applying the techniques she learned at AFI in her new business, Austin Images. Within a month she had finalized her business stationery, distributed her brochures in various business locations, sold a gift certificate for one hour of her time, had a press release published in three area newspapers, gave a seminar at a retirement village, completed two individual client consultations (10.5 hours) and was in the middle of two other individual consultations (7 - 8 hours each), and had booked four group seminars for the following month.

Jill wrote that the retirement village seminar resulted in 10 of the 12 ladies in the audience signing up for color analysis, and two more corporations and many other individuals were expressing interest in her services. "I have hardly had a chance to catch my breath," she wrote." Things are going great. This could easily be full-time if I wanted. I am having a ball. Satisfied customers are so motivational!" Keep in mind that this was all in the first month! Obviously, Jill is a real go-getter.

• **SANDRA LANGHORNE** lives in Winnipeg, Canada. After getting a bachelor's degree with majors in zoology and statistics, she worked for nearly ten years as an employment counselor and facilitator for the city of Winnipeg's Social Services Department before deciding to go for what she really loved: counseling on fashion and image.

Sandra received her certification through AFI's Home Study Program. She had business cards printed—very conservative, designed to appeal to corporations and public organizations. She was already a board member of the Manitoba Association of Learning Facilitators and joined the Women Business Owners of Manitoba. Among her first clients were the YM/YWCA's Entrepreneurial Program and the University of Manitoba's Connect Program.

Instead of a brochure, Sandra created a prospectus on her professional development workshop series designed to "address the need to enhance communication and develop professional and personal skills of management and staff within the workplace." Among the workshops she gives: Dressing for Success—The Do's and Don'ts, Body Language—Presenting a Confident Image, Powerful Communication and Presentation Skills, Telecommunications Etiquette Training, Business Manners, and Business Dining.

• **LILLIAN JOHNSON** is also a graduate of the AFI Home Study Program. Before starting her Brooklyn, New York-based image consulting business, Creative Elegance, Lillian was with the Environmental Protection Agency, where she was honored with three bronze medals for her work in environmental education and community relations. After receiving her AFI certification she joined the

Association of Image Consultants, International and the National Association of Female Executives.

Lillian discovered that there was a critical need to provide professional image training for students who hold part-time jobs and for students planning to work their way through college. She is involved in the Suited for Success "School-to-Work" image training program in New York City, and has conducted professional image seminars for the East New York Urban Youth Corps, the Mid-Manhattan Adult Learning Center, and the New York City Board of Education. Lillian has provided training in several public high schools as part of the nationwide "School-to-Career" initiative. She is also senior instructor at the Academy of Fashion & Image.

§ *Summary of Do's and Don'ts*

• DON'T skip the training and certification process that separates the professionals from the unqualified amateurs in this field. DO invest the requisite time and money in becoming properly trained and affiliating yourself with a mentor.

• DON'T wait until everything is perfect before starting your business.

• DO take the time to write a Business Plan. (See Chapter 5.)

• DO seek advice from the Small Business Administration office in your area.

- DO invest in quality letterhead stationery and business cards.

- DON'T forget to look the part of a fashion and image consultant. "Being good is not enough; you have to look good too."

- DO join community and business organizations.

- DON'T try to turn friends into clients.

- DO consider offering some free services to get started.

- DO write press releases. (See Chapter 6 for tips.)

- DON'T be inflexible on fees. DO be willing to negotiate.

Notes

THE BUSINESS PLAN

§ *Elements of a Business Plan*

A business plan says, in effect, that you are ready to do the work to translate your dreams of becoming an image consultant into reality.

In the business plan, you identify your goals and objectives, the strategies you will employ, and the actions you will take—all within a designated time frame. In other words, you lay out what you want to accomplish and how and when you are going to do it. Typically, detailed business plans are developed for one year. Longer-term goals also may be addressed.

There is no one "right way" to develop a business plan. At the Academy of Fashion & Image, students are exposed to a variety of business plans to use as models. Most of these address specifics in the following areas:

- management/business aspects
- product/service development
- client development, marketing, public relations (addressed separately or together, since these areas overlap)
- finance/budget projections

§   Outline of a Typical Business Plan

Title Page:

NAME OF BUSINESS
NAME OF OWNER
ADDRESS AND PHONE NUMBER

Page One:

OVERVIEW/BUSINESS DESCRIPTION

- *Name of your business*
- *What services your business offers*
- *Your qualifications*
- *Mission statement (optional)*
- *What the business plan will cover*

Page Two:

I. BUSINESS MANAGEMENT

Goals & Strategies (*addressed
together or separately)*

- Basic Resources
    Office:
    - *Where will your office be located?*
    - *What equipment and supplies do you need to purchase?*

    Business Setup:
    - *What form is your business (sole proprietorship limited liability corporation, etc.)?*
    - *What accounting method will you use?*
    - *Where will you open a business checking account?*

    Assistance:
    - *Identify contractors and associates: Have you decided on an accountant? Are you planning to hire consultants/assistants or will you do everything yourself?*

- Policies and Procedures
  - *Where will services be rendered?*
  - *When is payment due?*

Timeline
    - *When will you accomplish the above items?*

Page Three:

II. SERVICES DEVELOPMENT

Goals & Strategies

- Products/Services and Charges

- Materials and Presentations

- Keeping Current:
  - *Identify/subscribe to newspapers and magazines to keep abreast of cultural, business, and fashion trends.*
  - *Identify associations and individuals in the field with whom you will network.*

Timeline
    - *When will you accomplish the above items?*

Page Four:

III. CLIENT-BASE DEVELOPMENT

Goals & Strategies

- Potential Clients
  - *How will you identify individuals and businesses who are potential customers? How will you approach them?*
- Client Files and Client Follow-up System
- Networking
  - *What local organizations will you consider joining?*

Timeline
- *When will you accomplish the above items?*

Page Five:

IV. PUBLICITY

Goals & Strategies

- Marketing Materials
  - *Brochure, press releases that will be developed in conjunction with specific events; other materials*

- Radio and Television Appearances

Timeline
- *When will you accomplish the above items?*

Page Six:

V. FINANCE/BUDGET PROJECTIONS

Projected Income

Projected Expenses

§ *Sample Business Plan*

Better Image, LLC
Susan Smith, Principal
1234 FIRST STREET
RIVERTON, OHIO 54321
012-345-6789

BUSINESS PLAN

OVERVIEW

BETTER IMAGE, LLC, is a limited liability corporation founded by Susan Smith. It will provide such services as color analysis, wardrobe planning, personal shopping, and other aspects of image development for individuals; also, seminars to groups and businesses on professional image, corporate protocol, job interview skills, and public speaking. In addition, personal coaching will be offered in speech, body language, social etiquette, and making presentations.

Susan Smith has a master's degree in speech and language, and has more than ten years of experience working with individuals and groups. She will be a graduate of the Academy of Fashion & Image and a certified image consultant when she completes her training in January.

This Business Plan will describe what is required during the coming year for Better Image to become an established image consulting practice. The emphasis will be on becoming known rather than on profit. Greater profitability is anticipated in subsequent years.

I. BUSINESS MANAGEMENT

GOALS & STRATEGIES

Basic Resources
- Better Image, LLC, will operate from my home. The facilities will be shared with my speech therapy practice. All equipment is in place. Supplies to be ordered: business cards and letterhead stationery, envelopes, and miscellaneous items.

- Consult with a certified public accountant to set up Better Image as a limited liability corporation in the state of Ohio. Get other relevant advice from the CPA.

- I will perform all administrative functions of the business myself during the first year.

Policies and Procedures
- Consultations are by appointment only. Most consultations will be at the client's location, although small groups for color analysis and some individuals may meet in my home. For individual clients, payment is due when services are rendered. For corporate clients, a down payment will be requested when the appointment is made, with the balance due the day the seminar is delivered.

TIMELINE

January
- Complete image consultant training at AFI.

February
- Consult with CPA, order business cards and stationery, set up office. Order periodical subscriptions.

II. SERVICES DEVELOPMENT

GOALS & STRATEGIES

Services
- Provide to individual clients at $75 an hour, or in package deals:
    - color analysis, figure analysis and clothing line and style, closet analysis, wardrobe plan, personal shopping
    - personal coaching in speech, body language, presentation skills, social etiquette, and business protocol

- Provide to businesses at $1,000 to $1,500 a day: seminars in professional image, corporate protocol, making presentations.

Materials and Presentations - Develop
- for individual consultations
- for corporate seminars
- for job interview image workshop with graduating seniors
- for adult education workshops
- for fashion show

Portfolio for Marketing Services - Develop, including
- names of corporate clients
- "before" and "after" photos of clients (get their permission)
- newspaper and magazine articles in which I am featured or mentioned, or that I have written

Keeping Current
- Subscribe to *Image Networker, Women's Wear Daily, The New York Times* (Sunday edition), *Business Week.*
- Attend meetings of local chapter of Association of Image Consultants, International (AICI).

TIMELINE - See Timeline for *III. CLIENT-BASE DEVELOPMENT*

III. CLIENT-BASE DEVELOPMENT

GOALS & STRATEGIES

Individuals
- Consult with 16 individual clients resulting from activities and events (as described in the timeline) and from referrals.

Paid Corporate Seminars
- Give four paid seminars as a minimum:
    - Conduct two at employment agencies or executive search firms. Predicated on successfully contacting and giving a seminar to one employment agency or executive search firm, and then building on the experience to give a seminar of the same type to a similar firm.

    - Following the methodology outlined for employment agencies, conduct seminars for two similar businesses or organizations. Focus on markets with potential for repeat business.

Paid Adult Education Workshops/Classes
- One to be given in the summer and one in the fall (see timeline for details)

Other Paid Workshops
- One workshop to be given to a singles group and one to a YWCA or other community group

Free Presentations
- seminar for graduating seniors at Riverton College
- speaking engagements at meetings of local organizations
- fashion show benefit for women's shelter

<u>Client Files</u>
- Develop and maintain files on potential clients and referrals.
- Develop a system for client follow-up.

<u>Networking</u>
- Attend and consider joining Chamber of Commerce, Business & Professional Women, Women Business Owners.

TIMELINE (Incorporates items from *II. SERVICES DEVELOPMENT*)

February
- Contact Riverton College's School of Business about giving seminar to graduating seniors in May.

- Attend monthly meetings of Chamber of Commerce, Business and Professional Women, and Women Business Owners. Offer to be a speaker.

- Research other business, trade, and community organizations looking for speakers at their meetings and conventions.

March
- Contact clothing store, women's shelter, and community center about presenting fall fashion show in September. Enlist shoe store, hairdresser, and makeup artist as well.

- Research recreational and educational facilities in which adult classes are held. Prepare and submit proposals for teaching a class in the summer on various aspects of image, in preparation for fall.

- Contact employment centers, executive search firms, and placement agencies about giving seminars on professional image.

- Prepare a list of local businesses/corporations. Call the human resources departments of these businesses to identify the appropriate persons to contact. Start sending letters at a rate of four a month. Follow up with telephone calls and offer to send proposals.

April
- Prepare proposal and give a seminar resulting from contact with employment agencies. (Expect one individual client to result.)

- Give a paid seminar to another employment agency. (Expect one individual client to result.)

- Conduct a color analysis session for four people – the two paying clients and two free participants whom I choose.

- Continue to contact businesses.

- Make a list of community organizations that might be interested in image seminars; e.g., singles groups, women's clubs, Kiwanis Club. Contact directors/presidents of these organizations.

May
- Prepare materials for and give seminar to graduating seniors at Riverton College. (Expect two individual clients to result.) Send follow-up letter offering to give seminar again, but for a fee.

- Provide wardrobe consultation, shopping services, and personal coaching to prepare the two clients resulting from the college seminars for job interviews.

- Give a paid seminar for a corporation. (Expect one individual consultation as a result.)

- Prepare proposals to a singles group and the YWCA.

- Provide a wardrobe consultation to one individual resulting from the corporate seminar.

June
- Provide wardrobe consultation, shopping services, and personal coaching to prepare two clients resulting from press releases for job interviews (see *IV. PUBLICITY*).

- Teach an adult education workshop/class on image. (Expect one individual client to result.)

- Prepare proposals to a singles group and the YWCA.

- Continue to contact businesses and attend meetings.

July
- Provide wardrobe consultation to one client resulting from the adult education workshop.

- Continue to contact businesses, associations, and groups.

- Intensify preparations for fashion show benefit in September.

August
- Continue to work on fashion show benefit. Talk to producer of a local television program about the event and offer to put on a televised fashion show.

- Schedule personal shopping for the July client when fall fashions arrive in the stores.

September
- Give makeovers to residents of the women's shelter. Coordinate and narrate the fashion show benefit for the women's shelter. (Expect two individual clients to result.) Narrate fashion show for television program segment. (Expect two individual clients to result.)

- Schedule the four individual consultations resulting from the fashion show, TV show, and press releases. Conduct color analysis group session for the four clients.

- Teach adult education workshop/class on some aspect of image. (Expect one individual client to result.)

October
- Give a paid presentation to a singles group. (Expect two individual clients to result.)

- Schedule three individual clients—one from the adult education workshop, two from the singles group.

November
- Speak at a meeting of a community organization.

- Give a paid business seminar. (Expect two individual clients to result.)

- Schedule two individual clients from the business seminar and one referral.

- Give a paid presentation at the YWCA.

December
- Sell gift certificates for services.

SUMMARY

Individual Clients		Corporate/Group Clients
2 in April	4 in Sept.	2 in April
3 in May	3 in Oct.	2 in May (1 full fee, 1 free)
2 in June	3 in Nov.	1 in June (reduced fee)
1 in July	**18 individuals**	1 in Sept. (reduced fee)
		2 in Nov. (1 full fee, 1 reduced)
Special Events		**8 groups**
1 fashion show, 1 TV show		

IV. PUBLICITY

GOALS, STRATEGIES, AND TIMELINE

- Develop brochure. *(February)*

- Send four press releases:
  - one announcing that Better Image is open for business *(February)*

  - one on projecting the right image at job interview—send immediately after the seminar given at Riverton College *(May)*

  - two in conjunction with the fall fashion benefit for the women's shelter—one announcing the event and another providing more detail just before the event
  - *(August/September)*

- Appear on local television program in conjunction with fall fashion show. *(September)*

- Offer to write occasional, exclusive feature articles on some aspect of image for a local newspaper. *(October)*

- Research industry newsletters and other publications and propose to write articles. *(Throughout the year)*

V. FINANCE/BUDGET PROJECTIONS

INCOME

- Eighteen individual consultations:
  - Fourteen consultations involving color analysis, wardrobe planning, and personal shopping - @ estimated $350 ea. $6,300

  - Four consultations involving color, wardrobe, and personal coaching for job interviews – @ estimated $400 ea.

- Two business seminars - @ estimated $1,500 ea.   3,000

- Two seminars for employment agencies @ estimated $1,000 ea.   2,000

- Two adult education workshops @ estimated $500 ea.   1,000

- Workshop for singles group (30 people) and YWCA (30 people) @ $20 each   <u>1,200</u>
       $15,100

EXPENSES

Brochure	$ 250
Business cards, letterhead, envelopes	65
Printing & office supplies	200
Subscriptions	150
Association memberships	200
CPA and legal services	350
Liability insurance	150
Telephone	360
Color drapes, swatches, visual aides, training materials	<u>400</u>
	$2,125

§ A Flexible Document

A business plan is a guide that can and should be reviewed and changed as often as necessary to reflect the way the business is shaping up and the direction in which you want to go. Much of the business plan, particularly during the first year, is based on projections that may or may not materialize. Real outcomes may cause you to rethink assumptions and modify some of your goals and strategies.

For example, Susan Smith's strategy in the first four months of her business practice is to attract individual clients looking for jobs. Whether or not this strategy works will depend partly on the economic conditions in the country at the time and whether it is a job seeker's or an employer's market. Fortunately Susan is casting a wider net as well by contacting a variety of businesses and organizations.

It may turn out that Susan will be inundated by clients seeking advice on polishing their image for job interviews, as a result of her seminars at the college and the employment agencies, and referrals from satisfied clients. If that happens, she may choose to postpone some of her other planned activities, such as the adult education workshop.

On the other hand, she may find that job seekers are so confident in a booming market they aren't willing to pay for advice on image. If that turns out to be the case, Susan may decide to turn her focus in another direction.

Susan's business plan recognizes that it will take a while to establish herself as an image consultant. She does not expect to have any clients right away while she gets the word out. Her business plan also reflects an understanding of the requirement for advance planning by starting in March to make the contacts and lay the groundwork for a fashion benefit in September.

The first year is a time for trying this and that, for exploring different avenues and not becoming discouraged if one avenue doesn't work out. If the fledgling consultant has been adequately prepared by her trainer and mentor, her expectations will be realistic and she can weather whatever disappointments she may experience.

6 SOME TRICKS OF THE TRADE

§ *Writing Press Releases*

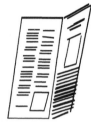

Most people care about how they look. The smart image consultant takes advantage of this by writing an occasional press release about some aspect of fashion and/or image, weaving in mention of her name and expertise. Written in the third person, this type of release is more apt to be picked up by weekly community newspapers than by large metropolitan dailies. The chances it will be published are increased if it is tied in with an upcoming or recent event.

In the example on the following page, note that our fictional image consultant Susan Smith timed her release to coincide with an impending graduation at the local college. Note, too, that within the release she refers to a recent workshop she gave to graduating college seniors on preparing for the job interview, thereby reinforcing that she is an expert on the subject.

Instead of sending the release to all the local papers, Susan could have offered it to just one newspaper as an exclusive. If the newspaper accepted it, Susan could propose to write other exclusive feature stories from time to time under her byline. In fact, this release could have been written as a feature story by changing from the third person to the first person.

Better Image, LLC
1234 FIRST STREET
RIVERTON, OHIO 54321   **PRESS RELEASE**

For more information, contact
Susan Smith at 012-345-6789   For Immediate Release

ATTENTION GRADUATES:
POLISH YOUR IMAGE BEFORE THE JOB INTERVIEW

The days are longer, the roses are budding, and soon the class of 2001 will be leaving college and looking for jobs. But before the graduates can enter the work force, there is the matter of the dreaded job interview.

Remember the saying, "You don't get a second chance to make a first impression?" Most prospective employers judge an applicant within seconds of meeting him/her. If the first impression is negative, it will be hard to overcome because the employer will be on the alert throughout the interview to confirm his initial judgment.

"A crucial element in preparing for a job interview is knowing what kind of image you want to project, and then taking the steps to ensure you project that image," says Susan Smith of Better Image, LLC, an image consulting firm.

According to Smith, part of being prepared for a job interview is doing what your mother always told you to do: comb your hair, brush your teeth, tuck in your shirt, and don't slouch. The applicant should always be dressed neatly; no frayed sleeves, missing buttons, torn hems, or scuffed shoes.

Appearance also encompasses body language—the signals you send by the way you hold and move your body. "When your prospective employer introduces himself and offers a handshake, reach out and clasp his hand firmly, smile warmly, and make eye contact," Smith advises. "Smile often during the interview and keep your head up. Look directly into the employer's eyes while talking. Avoid nervous gestures—no rattling change, clicking a pen, or fidgeting with your hair. What you want to convey is confidence and self-assurance."

- more -

Better Image, LLC

Advice to Graduating Seniors - Page 2

What to wear to the interview will depend on the type of business and the job you are applying for. Smith proposes spending a lunch hour at the company you want to work for. "Stand outside the building and notice how people are dressed when they go out for lunch," she suggests. "If the building is a high-rise, ride the elevator a few times. When people get on the elevator from the floor where the company is located, try to guess what position they hold in the company."

Banks, law firms, and many corporations require conservative dress, so applicants should dress accordingly. The conservative look for the interview is appropriate for other white-collar businesses as well, even if the work atmosphere is more informal. Prospective employers expect you to show up for the interview looking your business-like best. For men this means a suit (preferably dark blue or dark to medium gray); long-sleeved, white or solid-color shirt; tie in a solid color or pin dot, repp, or foulard pattern; a dark belt in a narrow to medium width with a conventional buckle; dark, shined shoes with laces; and dark, over-the-calf-socks.

For women, an appropriate conservative look is a dark, solid-color suit cut along classic lines with a contrasting blouse, or a dress with a matching jacket in a solid, neutral color; flesh-toned or seasonally appropriate dark hosiery, and low- to medium-heeled pumps (no white). The skirt should fit properly and not be too tight, with the hem length at the knee or slightly above or below. "Think decorum," Smith counsels. "No cleavage, dangling jewelry, or exaggerated makeup. Wear only one pair of earrings, clear nail polish, and no more than one ring on each hand."

Smith recently completed a workshop with graduating seniors at Riverton College School of Business. "At first, some of the students believed the way they dressed wasn't all that important to getting a job," Smith remarked. "Then I told them about a survey in which 84 out of 100 executives admitted that their companies had rejected applicants based solely on how they were dressed. That got their attention."

###

Another type of press release is the news release. It is trickier to write and harder to get published because it must meet a newspaper editor's test of news-worthiness without appearing to be a ploy to get publicity without paying for an ad. The best news release has a news "hook" that piques the interest of a newspaper editor or reporter and leads to an interview that will boost your visibility. Usually this type of release is not printed verbatim, although quotes from the release may be used.

Five Tips for Writing Press Releases

1. Write a press release about an aspect of fashion and/or image that is of interest to a significant segment of a local newspaper's readership, and time it with an upcoming or recent event.

2. Mention yourself and your services in the press release, but don't make that the focus.

3. Keep the paragraphs short.

4. Use quotes liberally.

5. After a couple of your press releases are printed in a local newspaper, approach the editor and offer to write occasional, exclusive, bylined articles about various aspects of fashion, personal appearance, and image enhancement.

§ *Using Your Time Effectively in Wardrobe Consulting*

When you are doing what you love, particularly when you are just starting out, you may be tempted not to pay attention to the clock. But if you want to make a living at image consulting, you have to treat it as a business, and that means learning to work within time constraints. When you set up an appointment with an individual client, tell him/her how long it will take and what the fee will be. The following are suggested timeframes for providing basic wardrobe consulting services.

WARDROBE CONSULTING SERVICES

Initial Interview for Wardrobe Assessment *(Often client is not charged for this time.)*	15-30 min.
Color Analysis *(Do if the client's best colors haven't been determined previously.)*	30 min.
Wardrobe Assessment *(Go through clothing in client's closet.)*	2 hours
Wardrobe Proposal	2 hours
Preview Shopping	2 hours
Shopping with Client	2 hours

• Wardrobe Assessment - Initial Interview

When you set up the appointment to do a wardrobe analysis, tell the client that it will take approximately 2-1/2 hours and that you will do only one seasonal combination: fall/winter or spring/summer. Make sure the client understands that fees are due at the end of the appointment.

So that you can go through the clothes quickly (and save the client money), ask that the client do some organizing before you get there: put out-of-season items at one end of the closet or in another closet; remove clothes worn around the house or put them with the out-of-season clothes, lay out belts, jewelry, and scarves on the bed; line up shoes and handbags outside the closet.

Bring two copies of a questionnaire to the client's home, one for you and one for the client. An alternative time-saving suggestion is to send the client a copy of the questionnaire to fill out before you arrive. Spend a few minutes making your client feel comfortable. Explain how the consultation works and how this service can save time and money. Mention other services you offer. To help you determine the client's needs, go over the questionnaire.

SAMPLE QUESTIONNAIRE FOR PROFESSIONALS

Name _____ Home phone _____

Home address _____

Company name _____ Phone _____

Company address _____

Your

Profession _____ Position _____ Supervise others? _____

Professional goals _____

How does your supervisor dress? _____

How do the senior executives dress? _____

How do others in your office dress? _____

How do you think others in the office perceive you (image)? _____

_____

Do you have concerns about your clothes and/or appearance? Describe.

_____

What image would you like to project? _____

What message do you want to send to others about you? (Check all that apply.)

☐ Refined   ☐ Authoritative   ☐ Competitive   ☐ Successful
☐ Athletic   ☐ Casual   ☐ Intelligent   ☐ Friendly
☐ Conservative ☐ Believable   ☐ Creative   ☐ Efficient
☐ Poised   ☐ Command attention ☐ Artistic

Does your job require travel? _____ To what part(s) of the country/world?

_____

Frequency?_____ Season(s)? _____

Climate(s)? _____

QUESTIONNAIRE, Continued

Do you do business and/ or social entertaining? _____

What type? _____

Describe your lifestyle _____

_____

How do you spend your non-work time? _____

_____

Type of clothes you like _____

_____

Type of clothes you dislike _____

_____

What clothing stores do you shop in? _____

_____

Describe your clothes shopping habits _____

_____

_____

How much money are you currently spending per season on clothes? (Estimate)

_____

What would you like to get from this consultation? _____

_____

_____

_____

• **Wardrobe Assessment - Closet Analysis**

Categorize wardrobe items in the closet by color. Break up suits into jackets, skirts, pants. Put together all blouses/shirts, jackets, pants, skirts, dresses, etc. Show how new combinations appear as you do this. Try to establish a color scheme with basic colors and accent colors. Throughout the wardrobe evaluation, give the client tips on what to look for to get maximum value out of a wardrobe, how to organize clothing in the closet, and how to avoid spending a lot of money updating the present wardrobe.

Encourage the client to give away or sell those things that haven't been worn in two years, are out of style, don't fit, or are the wrong color or style. Ask the client to try on clothing you have doubts about. Never say anything negative about the client's wardrobe choices. Find something to compliment, and then tactfully suggest an alternative for the client to consider. Help the client to make a pile of items to eliminate, so that when you leave the closet is cleaned out.

Pull out items that still work and begin to assemble outfits. Hang items on a door or lay them across the bed. You will need a clear space to work. When an outfit is put together, pull accessories to finish the look, including scarves, belts, shoes, hosiery, and handbag. Make notes about core wardrobe combinations. I prefer to record them onto a small tape recorder as I work, and then transfer them later to a wardrobe inventory chart for the client. List wardrobe needs as well.

SAMPLE WARDROBE CHART

Item	Have	Need
Coats *(color)*		
Jackets *(color, pattern, style)*		
Suits *(color, pattern, style)*		
Skirts *(color, pattern, style)*		
Slacks, Shorts *(color)*		
Blouses, Tops *(color, style)*		
Sweaters *(color, style)*		
Dresses *(color, pattern, style)*		

SAMPLE WARDROBE CHART, CONTINUED

Item	Have	Need
P.M. Dressing *(color, style)*		
Jewelry *(color, type)*		
Belts *(color, style)*		
Handbags, Briefcase *(color, type)*		
Shoes, Boots *(color, style)*		
Socks, Hosiery		
Hats		

SAMPLE COORDINATION SHEET

Item of clothing _____

Goes with:

Jackets	Shoes, Handbags
Blouses/Tops/Sweaters	Scarves, Jewelry
Skirts, Slacks	Other

Continue to assemble outfits until you have incorporated all of the good pieces in the closet and illustrated various ways the client can wear them. Experiment with color combinations. Do not try to force changes she/he is not comfortable with. Instead, show which combinations are best so the client knows what to aim for.

At the end of session tell the client you will transfer your notes to wardrobe inventory charts which you will mail to her. Mention that you are available to prepare a wardrobe proposal as well as do personal shopping, and leave literature describing these services.

§ *Wardrobe Planning for Men*

The beginning female image consultant (and most are females) often gravitates toward other women as clients and avoids seeking out male clients. While this is understandable, it also is a mistake. Half the population is men, and they usually make wonderful clients. Perhaps because his mother picked out his clothes when he was growing up, a man seldom feels threatened by a female giving him professional advice on his wardrobe. Not only is he willing to trust her judgment, but his gratitude may be such that the experience becomes a major ego boost for her.

• *Closet Analysis.* There's one area I recommend you approach with caution, and that's the closet analysis, because it takes place in the man's bedroom. If you don't know the man very well, it's best to err on the side of caution and take an assistant with you.

If the man is married, set up a time when his wife will be present, although this can present another problem. Your client is likely to be among the 80 percent of men whose wardrobes have been selected by women, and in this case, that woman will probably be his wife. Since she is the one who selected the clothing you are suggesting be replaced, you are in a situation that requires the utmost diplomacy.

You may look upon this as either an interesting challenge or as a sticky wicket you want to avoid. If your reaction is the latter, give your client the wardrobe analysis instructions and charts to fill out himself and concentrate on the wardrobe proposal and wardrobe shopping for him.

PRESENT WARDROBE – MEN

Sport Coats	Trousers
Suits	**Shirts**
Accessories	
	Ties
Coats	

• *Wardrobe Plan.* The first step in planning the wardrobe for a male client is to set up an appointment for an initial interview and color analysis. This will take about an hour. During the interview go over a questionnaire similar to the unisex "Sample Questionnaire for Professionals." If your services will include shopping, a supplemental questionnaire, similar to the following, should be filled out.

SUPPLEMENTAL QUESTIONNAIRE FOR MEN

<u>Sizes:</u>

Sport Coat _____ **Trousers** _____ **Suit** _____ **Coat** _____

Shirt sleeve _____ **Shirt collar** _____ **Hat** _____ **Gloves** _____

Tie _____

Body Type _____

Special areas _____

Height _____ **Weight** _____ **Hair** _____ **Eyes** _____

Skin/undertone _____ **Color season** _____

Best colors _____

_____

---

§ *How to Shop*

Whether you are shopping for clothing for a man or a woman, the same suggestions apply. Don't wait until you have a client to visit clothing stores. Check out the merchandise several times each season, taking note of the styles, colors, fabrics, and trends.

Visit the designer areas to help develop your eye and sense of style and to recognize "knock offs"—copies of originals that sell for a fraction of the originals' cost.

Learn the layout of the stores that are the most promising. Locate the sections for petites and larger sizes. Determine the most successful designers and manufacturers by the amount of square footage they occupy and their location. Don't neglect the men's department.

While you are looking around, notice which sales associates seem particularly helpful and ask for their cards. You may want to consider introducing yourself to the managers in the departments you particularly like. Ask to be put on mailing lists for catalogs, special promotions, and sales.

• *Researching a Wardrobe in Two Hours.* Since you are already familiar with the stores in your area, you should be able to shop for an entire seasonal wardrobe in two hours. Shop when you are rested and shop for just one client at a time. Take with you the client's wardrobe proposal and the outline of his/her present wardrobe. Explain to the sales associate what you are doing. Pull the items and put them on hold.

• *Shopping with a Client.* Call the client and make an appointment to meet him/her in a specific area of the store. Ask the sales associate to set aside a large dressing room for the appointment. If possible, try to set up a time when the same sales associate will be there, particularly if he/she works on commission.

Establishing a good working relationship with store personnel will pay off in the future.

When the client arrives, show him/her what you have selected and observe his/her response before you become too enthusiastic. Have the client try on the item he/she likes best first, and be completely honest about how it looks on the client. If you think it doesn't work, say so. Ask the sales staff for assistance with sizes, accessories, etc. Try to read your client's reactions to your selections. Ask questions such as, "How do you like the style? Color? Fabric? Is it comfortable? Do **you** like it?" This process should take no more than two hours and should be a pleasant experience for you both.

§ *Ten Additional Tips for Success*

1. Build a portfolio. Keep track of all the publicity you get. Clip articles in which you are quoted as well as those you write that are published under your byline. Make a written record of television appearances, the name and date of the show and the name of the interviewer. Write down the name of every client. This information becomes part of your portfolio which helps you to market your services to other clients.

2. Plan and organize. Keep a good calendar handy and use it. Plan each day, each week, and each month. Learn how to keep records. Keep a notebook in your car to write down mileage. Record daily what you do, how much you spend on what, with whom you meet, decisions you make, and ideas for possible future use. Have a six-month plan, a one-year plan, and a five-year plan. Know where you are and where you are going.

3. Plan, but be flexible. Review your records and be ready to change your plans, to modify your expectations, to revise the outcomes. Accept disappointments. "No" is usually a rejection of your product or service, not a rejection of you personally. Remember that 49 percent "no" responses and 51 percent "yes" responses represent a positive majority.

4. Know your competition. Ascertain what other image consultants in your area are doing and what they are charging. Come up with ways to do it better or differently or more economically. If they have the experience you are seeking, consider hiring them as independent contractors. Keep your mind open. Let creative ideas surface. Be receptive to innovations. Be ready to try something new and different. Keep on learning.

5. Keep abreast of trends in business, cultural, physical fitness, health food, color, and fashion. Read *Women's Wear Daily, Business Week, Money, The N.Y. Times* Sunday edition, *O Magazine*, men's and women's magazines, and other periodicals.

6. Start at the top. If you get involved in fund raisers—something I recommend to become better known and to perform community service at the same time—don't be afraid to call people "at the top" with a request to speak or perform. They are usually approachable and open-minded. For example, I called Dr. Joyce Brothers directly when I wanted her as a keynote speaker for an association. Another time, when Dan Quayle was Vice President, I asked him if his wife, Marilyn, would be interested in giving a talk at a convention of the Association of Fashion and Image Consultants. As a result, she was the keynote speaker. If I had started at the bottom of the chain of command, I might not have been successful in getting these people.

7. Establish a support system. Surround yourself with a good team. Maintain supportive friendships and be supportive of your friends and colleagues in return.

8. Promptly return phone calls and messages. Answer all communications promptly and maintain your important contacts.

9. Keep your word. Build a good reputation. Deliver what you promise and on time.

10. Give your clients something extra. Clip ideas on wardrobe selection and maintenance, image, and related topics and type them up on "tip sheets" to give to your clients for reference. As a bonus for you, you can create articles based on these tip sheets.

Notes

CORPORATE LOOKS FOR THE 21ST CENTURY

§ *"Why Can't a Woman Be More Like a Man?"*

Professor Henry Higgins' lament in *My Fair Lady* was echoed in John Malloy's reaction when women began to repudiate his corporate uniform. Malloy first recommended the uniform in the 1970s, after observing the frustrations of women as they attempted to navigate the old-boy network in business.

Malloy wasn't suggesting that women try to look like men, but that they adopt a standard uniform that would instantly communicate "corporate professional," just as the traditional dark suit, white shirt, and tie do for men. The woman's uniform he devised consisted of a modified A-line skirt (or straight skirt, if it wasn't too sexy), a matching blazer in medium gray or dark blue worn with a high-contrast blouse. This was the look that would help women to establish an image of authority, he insisted.

Malloy's recommendation, based on solid research, was utterly logical. But it was also rooted in the typical male approach to dressing for work; i.e., tell me what the rules of dress are and I will happily conform to them, now and forevermore. For better or worse, that is not the typical female's approach to clothing. At first, women were willing to try the uniform for the sake of their careers, but after a while they abandoned it because they felt it made them look dowdy.

In addition, a new understanding of color's influence on personal appearance emerged in the 1980s. Malloy's recommendations about color did not consider skin undertones, which often determine which colors flatter and which do not. A woman with classic "autumn" coloring, for example, will look much better in suits of deep rust, aubergine, or dark brown than Malloy's recommended grays and blues.

§ Basically, Malloy Was Right

Nevertheless, the basic principles underlying Malloy's recommendations remain valid, and with some minor tweaking, are likely to do so throughout the 21st century.

1. Suits rule. The corporate uniform concept for women may be gone, but a classically tailored suit in a medium to dark color is still the outfit of choice for those occasions when the objective is to establish a look of authority. The same holds true for men. Softer looks for women, such as a tailored dress worn with a jacket, are appropriate for work days when looking authoritative is not paramount.

2. Don't confuse board room and bedroom looks. The corporate look for women is supposed to be businesslike, not sexy. If you've ever watched television soap operas, you may have been amused at Hollywood's idea of corporate dressing. Although the men wear traditional suits and ties, Tinseltown's idea of the corporate look for women accentuates cleavage, curves, and flash. In real life, women who occupy executive offices dress attractively, but tastefully and conservatively.

3. The corporate look is upper-middle class. Corporate executive positions are perceived as belonging to the upper-middle class. Therefore, to look the part of an executive, men and women must wear clothing that is identified with the upper-middle class. This means traditional styles, quality tailoring, and natural fabrics (or the look of natural fabrics). Anything flashy or trendy is to be avoided.

4. Dress for the job you want, not the job you have. While this recommendation is essentially correct, take heed of Emily Cho's counsel to "keep in mind that a lot of executives may have trouble with a super chic female. . . .You might do better with something a little less elegant and unfamiliar. Choose an outfit with impeccable details." The same advice holds true for men. Don't try to dress better than top management.

5. Dress appropriately for the locality. In the U.S. there are different norms of dress in regions, and in specific localities and metropolitan areas within regions. However, these distinctions are blurring as businesses move about seeking cheaper labor, lower taxes, better amenities, and for other reasons. The impact is two-way; that is, over time the transplanted company takes on some of the characteristics of the region, and businesses in the area take on some of the characteristics of the transplanted company, particularly if the company is a significant presence.

In general, the northeast part of the U.S.—the Boston, New York, Washington, D.C., corridor—is the most conservative. Dress is tailored, formal, authoritative. Colors tend toward dark neutrals. Dress in the South is traditional, but not so authoritative and hard-tailored as the Northeast. Fabrics are lighter and colors are brighter, as befits the warm, year-around climate.

Business clothing in the Midwest is traditional but not as formal as the Northeast. Darker colors are the norm, with brown being acceptable and even preferred in some areas. The most relaxed, informal business dress is worn in the Southwest. The West Coast has a range of semi-formal to formal traditional business dress, favoring the colors of the Northeast, except for Southern California, which has a mix of traditional and relaxed business clothing.

6. Dress appropriately for the industry. The degree of formality of dress depends in large measure upon the industry. In addition, each company within an industry may have its own preferred look. Finally, clothing worn by management within a specific company offers the best guide to follow.

GUIDE TO FORMALITY OF CORPORATE DRESS

Most Formal: *Applies to banks and other financial institutions, brokerage firms, corporate law offices.* Clothing is the most conservative, tailored, authoritative.

Men	Women
<u>Fall/Winter</u> • Traditional tailored suits in solid or pinstriped dark blue or gray wool • Long-sleeved, smooth cotton shirts with pointed or spread collars in solid white, white with thin pinstripes, and pale blue • Silk ties in dark solids, pin dot and foulard patterns, and regimental or repp stripes • Laced leather dress shoes such as wing-tips	<u>Fall/Winter</u> • Tailored, skirted suits in or coat dresses in dark, solid colors or pin-stripes, preferably navy or medium gray smooth wools, such as gabardine • Tailored silk blouses in solid colors • Outfit accessorized with a silk scarf and/or a pin and earrings • Leather pumps in neutral colors—such as black, navy, brown, or taupe—with low to medium heels
<u>Spring/Summer</u> • Tropical wool suits in medium gray and dark to medium blue • Long-sleeved cotton shirts with pointed or spread collars in white or pastels • Leather slip-on shoes (not loafers)	<u>Spring/Summer</u> • Tailored suits in tropical wool and silk doupionni in navy, medium blue, light to medium gray, and taupe or camel • Sheath-type dresses with matching jackets in the same fabrics and colors as for suits, plus linen-blends • Leather pumps in neutral colors

Semi-Formal 1: *Public relations, advertising, and insurance firms, some sales.* More options are acceptable, but still in the traditional range.

Men	Women
Fall/Winter	**Fall/Winter**
• Wool suits in a herringbone pattern are acceptable, in addition to smooth textures	• Knit suits, wool dresses worn with jackets, preferably in dark, neutral colors
• Long-sleeved, smooth cotton shirts with pointed or spread collars in whites and pastels	• Silk blouses in rich prints in addition to solid colors
Spring/Summer	**Spring/Summer**
• Tropical wool suits in muted plaids are acceptable. Lighter shades of neutral colors are acceptable, including tan	• Suits and jacketed dresses in silk twill and linen blends
	• Blouses in prints and solids, in tissue linen, cotton, and rayon

Semi-Formal 2: *Government agencies, government contractors, some sales.* Dress code is more relaxed, but not casual. Top executives may dress more formally.

Men	Women
Fall/Winter	**Fall/Winter**
• Suits more informal in style; worn with solid-color, button-down shirts and striped ties	• Unmatched separates such as a solid-color wool skirt worn with a coordinating houndstooth check jacket
	• Softer, fuller skirts with jackets; knit dresses
	• Tailored wool pants suits
Spring/Summer	Spring/Summer
• Cotton and cotton/blend suits in addition to tropical wools, in lighter neutral colors	• Silk and rayon print dresses and skirts with solid-color jackets
	• Skirted suits, dresses, and pant suits in silk noile, linen, cotton, and blends

GUIDE TO MEN'S TRADITIONAL
DRESS STANDARDS

SUITS

Fabrics: Standard is wool (tropical wool for summer) or wool blends.

Colors: Dark colors are considered the most conservative and authoritarian, with dark blue and medium gray to dark gray the standard colors for winter. Brown is acceptable in parts of the Midwest. Medium blues and grays and shades of tan (from taupe to camel) are standard colors for summer.

Jacket: Standard American style is single-breasted, with low-cut armholes, two-button closure, and center-back vent. Notched lapel is 3-1/4 to 3-1/2 inches at widest part. Sufficient length to cover buttocks. Set-in pockets with flaps are standard. (Patch pockets are considered casual.) Sleeves hit middle of wrist bone.

Trousers: Pleated or plain front. Trouser leg is no wider than 20 inches in circumference at the bottom. Trouser leg length breaks slightly at top of shoe in front. Longer in back to hit top of the shoe heel. No cuffs, as cuffs are considered casual.

- continued -

SHIRTS

Fabric: Cotton or cotton blends. Look for long-staple, combed cotton in smooth broadcloth. Egyptian and Sea Island are the smoothest, followed by pima cotton. (Oxford and pinpoint oxford cloth are slightly textured and are considered informal.)

Color: White is standard, followed by pale blue.

Collar: Straight pointed collar is standard. Spread collar is also acceptable. (Button-down collar is considered informal and is worn with sport coats.)

Sleeves: Long sleeves are standard. (Short sleeves are considered casual and are not worn with suits.) Barrel style, 3-inch-wide button cuffs are standard and are meant to protrude 1/2 to 3/4 inch beyond jacket sleeves. French cuffs are the dressiest type of cuff.

ACCESSORIES

Belts should be 1" to 1-1/4" wide, in black or brown, with inconspicuous gold or silver buckles.

Shoes to wear with business suits are thin-soled leather lace ups and unadorned slip-ons (not loafers).

Socks should be dark and fit over the calf.

Jewelry should be limited to a gold or silver watch and a wedding ring.

TIES

<u>Width</u>: A tie should be the same width as the widest point of the jacket lapel. Since the lapel on a standard suit is approximately 3-1/4 to 3-1/2 inches, that should be the width of tie with which it is worn.

<u>Length</u>: The tip of the tie should brush the top of the trouser belt buckle.

<u>Fabric/Color/Pattern</u>: Silk is the preferred tie fabric for business dress. In general, the color of the tie should be darker than the shirt but lighter than the suit. The more colors there are in a tie, the more informal it is. The safest tie for business is of solid-color silk. Regimental or repp striped ties are considered power ties for daytime business wear and also can be worn with sport coats. Other patterns to wear with suits are the pin dot (the most formal and appropriate for evening wear as well) and the "Ivy League" foulard (a tiny repeating pattern against a solid background).

Paisley, club, and plaid patterns are informal and should not be worn with traditional business suits. Cotton and wool ties are strictly for casual wear.

§ *Revenge of the Nerds*

Your clients are conscientiously following the image rules in the corporate world when they read that yet another young computer expert has just made millions of dollars from the company he started in his father's garage. The newspaper photo shows the

smiling youngster wearing a t-shirt, faded jeans, no socks, and worn sneakers. So much for dressing for success!

There have always been those who thumb their noses at the rules and rise to the top anyway by believing in themselves and by being very good at what they do. Besides, there's a poetic justice in the triumph of the supposedly "uncool." Today's newest millionaires and billionaires aren't the superstar athletes but those once labeled nerds and geeks, who applied their understanding of computer technologies to achieve stunning successes.

Nevertheless, the youthful exuberance and nonconformity of these whiz-kids inevitably fades. After a while, the computer generation wants to be taken seriously and join the grown-ups. "We don't want to be a bunch of kids and computers anymore, and we realized there was a disconnect with the world we moved in, " Chan Suh, co-owner of an Internet marketing and design firm told *The New York Times*. And that means putting on suits, shirts and ties, and polished leather shoes. It means knowing business and social protocols. It means hiring image consultants so that they get it right!

§   The Business Casual Phenomenon

In 1991, when the Aluminum Company of America (ALCOA) granted a "dress down day" to its employees who contributed to the United Way, it started a trend that by the late 1990's was adopted in some fashion by 87 percent of offices in the United

States, including such conservative institutions as banks, brokerage companies, and law firms. According to a survey done for Levi Strauss & Co., corporate policies range from allowing dress down days occasionally, to one day a week (usually Fridays), to five days a week. In 1998, approximately half of U.S. office workers were being allowed to dress casually during the entire work week.

Proponents of casual dress in the workplace cite improved morale and better camaraderie with managers and co-workers. Some say that a relaxed dress code improves productivity, although others say that the increased productivity may be due to workers spending more time behind their desks and avoiding appointments with clients on casual dress day.

Perhaps the biggest beneficiary of casual business dress has been the retail clothing industry, which had been in a slump during the economic recession that started in the late 1980's and continued into the early 1990's. (Although business casual has hurt traditional men's wear clothiers who did not adapt.) Image consultants, who also suffered from the recession, found a new niche in advising corporations and individual employees about acceptable casual clothing in the workplace.

However, the uncertainty over what to wear on casual dress day—the same uncertainty that has brought image consultants business—has led to some employee complaints and even requests to discontinue dress down practices altogether. Men soon discovered that "casual" does not necessarily mean the comfortable clothing they wear on weekends; that "relaxed" does not mean old jeans, t-shirts, and sneakers. Some have had to purchase additional wardrobes just to meet dress down requirements.

Women have expressed concern that casual attire has diminished their hard-won authority, and yet they cannot opt out of casual day and still be perceived as team players. Other women have complained that they cannot afford to buy the more expensive casual clothes worn by higher-paid female employees, thereby further diminishing their status at the office.

Because casual isn't considered appropriate attire in which to meet clients, employees may have to keep a change of clothes handy for unexpected client meetings that occur on dress down days.

Despite the problems that have cropped up, it is likely that the trend toward informal dress in the office will continue at least on some days, particularly in the summer. Keeping in mind that dress codes will vary from company to company, some suggestions follow. Examples are included for those with cool undertones to their skin (winters and summers) and warm undertones (springs and autumns).

SUGGESTIONS FOR FORMAL BUSINESS CASUAL

Think conservative, upper-middle class casual. Sport coats and slacks for men, separates for women. Some conservative corporations may frown on pants suits and slacks for women. Wools in solid colors and tweeds; cashmere and merino wool and cotton knits for sweaters. Summer fabrics include linen, cotton, and raw silk noile. Footwear: leather loafers for men, flats or low heel pumps for women.

Men	
Fall/Winter	Spring/Summer
• Gray and black tweed jacket and medium gray flannel slacks -- with light gray cotton shirt and solid maroon or solid medium gray tie (summers) -- with pure white or ice pink cotton shirts and maroon/gray/white striped tie (winters) • Camel's hair jacket, navy slacks, and light camel shirt -- with rust v-neck sweater and rust/navy/camel striped tie (autumns) -- with clear, medium blue shirt and blue/camel/navy striped tie (springs)	• Navy blazer and tan slacks -- with ice blue shirt and tie with club design on a deep blue background (winters) • Dusty blue hopsack jacket and tan slacks -- with soft white shirt and deep blue tie with foulard pattern in blue/maroon/white (summers) • Gray cotton poplin suit -- with pale yellow shirt and solid yellow or solid gray tie (springs) -- with light raspberry shirt and deep raspberry tie (winters and summers) • Tan cotton poplin suit -- with medium blue shirt and Thai silk tie in muted blue/yellow/pink plaid (springs and summers) -- with yellow shirt and Thai silk tie (springs)

Women	
Fall/Winter	Spring/Summer

• Medium gray jacket, skirt, and pants
 	
  -- with black turtleneck sweater, or crisp white shirt and black vest (winters)
 	
  -- with grayed navy sweater, or light gray blouse and navy vest (summers)
 	
• Brown and camel check cardigan jacket and matching slacks, dark brown slacks, dark brown sweater and camel sweater (autumns)
 	
• Coral wool jacket, dove gray sweater, and muted gray plaid slacks (springs)
	• Cocoa brown silk noile sheath dress and matching jacket with scarf in cocoa, soft white, and rose-pink pattern (summers)
	
	• Aqua silk broadcloth shirtwaist with camel raw silk jacket (springs)
	
	• Aubergine linen-blend jacket with forest green linen-blend pants and blouse in aubergine, forest green, and cream stripes (autumns)
	
	• Medium gray linen-cotton jacket and cuffed Bermuda shorts (worn with hose) and turquoise shirt (winters)

SUGGESTIONS FOR SEMI-FORMAL BUSINESS CASUAL

Less conservative styles and fabrics are acceptable. **For men:** tweed sport coats, corduroy slacks and jackets, cotton slacks and jackets, sport shirts in solids and muted plaids with ties optional. Worn with loafers (not sneakers). Some companies may allow dark, pressed jeans and cotton knit polo shirts in solid colors. **For women:** Pants suits, casual slacks, and skirts with unstructured jackets. Cotton knit dresses, soft shirtwaist dresses and skirts in solids and sophisticated prints, all worn with tailored jackets. Low-heeled pumps or flats.

- continued -

Men	
<u>Fall/Winter</u>	<u>Spring/Summer</u>
• Navy and gray herringbone tweed sport coat and gray pinwale corduroy slacks	• Khaki cotton slacks and jacket
-- with navy turtleneck sweater (winters)	-- with ice pink button-down shirt and deep pink cotton tie (winters)
-- with maroon v-neck sweater, white shirt, and maroon/navy/gray striped tie (winters)	-- with light blue denim shirt and cotton tie in a dusty blue/rose/tan/white plaid (summers)
-- with gray shirt and gray tie (summers)	-- with light golden tan shirt and paisley tie in tan/brown/ cream/yellow (springs)
• Dark brown and camel tweed sport coat	-- with light golden brown shirt and deep gold tie (autumns)
-- with dark brown corduroy slacks, burnt orange shirt, camel crew neck sweater and dark camel tie with orange/gold/ cream paisley design (autumns)	
-- with camel corduroy slacks and orange-red sweater (springs)	

Women	
<u>Fall/Winter</u>	<u>Spring/Summer</u>
• Cherry red gabardine blazer with silver turtleneck sweater, and black corduroy slacks (winters)	• Black and white glen plaid cotton-linen jacket with white oxford cloth shirt and black denim skirt (winters)
• Gray flannel blazer and slacks with plum turtleneck sweater (summers)	• Rose linen jacket with celadon green cotton knit top and rayon print soft skirt in shades of rose, celadon, and moss green (summers)
• Lime green twin sweater set with clear navy slacks (springs)	
• Mustard gold and brown herringbone blazer, bronze shirt, and dark bronze corduroy slacks (autumns)	• Khaki and cream striped jacket in polished cotton with khaki linen-blend slacks and bright yellow shirt (springs)
	• Unstructured cotton jacket in brown, cream, gold, and rust plaid over cream shirt and rust cotton slacks (autumns)

Summary. Corporate casual clothing is more relaxed than what is usually worn in the business environment. Manufacturers use terms such as "city casual" and "dress sportswear" to describe the style. Summer dress is usually more casual and unstructured than in the winter. The degree of casual allowed varies with the formality of the corporate culture of specific industries and companies. Management sets the tone, and employees are advised not to dress more informally than the managers at their company.

Examples of inappropriate business casual

Corporate casual is not weekend casual. The following are not considered appropriate for the business environment: sweatsuits, athletic wear, workout clothing, beachwear, cutoffs or shorts, sweat shirts or t-shirts with printed messages, loud clothing, distressed clothing, and anything dirty, torn, or rumpled. Many companies do not consider sneakers and open-toe sandals appropriate.

Women should add to the above list anything too tight, too revealing, too glamorous, or too trendy. Mini-skirts, hotpants, leggings, and tank tops are no-no's.

> **RULE OF THUMB:**
>
> If you jog in it, bike in it, go to the beach in it, mow the lawn in it, wash the car in it, lounge in it, sleep in it, go dancing or to a cocktail lounge in it, don't wear it to work!

§ As the World Gets Smaller

One trend that will curtail the adoption of business casual dress five days a week in many U.S. companies is the continuing expansion into global markets. Accepted business dress in international circles is formal in tone, and therefore casual dress risks alienating potential customers. The computer makes doing global business easier, but will not completely erase the need for face to face communications. Increased international business travel also creates a niche for image consultants to advise on travel wardrobes, smart packing, and business and social protocols in other cultures.

§ Telecommuting

Imagine getting out of bed, having a cup of coffee, and then getting down to work making phone calls, researching on the Internet, and otherwise taking care of business while still in your pajamas. Technology has made telecommuting a reality for an increasing number of people, and the trend will continue to grow in the 21st century. Although business clothes are still required for meetings with clients and visits to corporate headquarters, the telecommuter's wardrobe usually can be smaller. This means that higher quality clothing becomes more affordable, especially if image consultants are hired to ensure cost-effectiveness.

§ *What about Image Consultants' Wardrobes?*

"The key to chic is appropriateness," Emily Cho wrote over 25 years ago. "Always keep in mind who you are, who your audience is going to be, and what you want to project to that audience. " That is particularly good advice for people who make their living in sales, including image consultants, who sell their expertise based in large part on their appearance. Image consultants must communicate both authority and accessibility to specific audiences. This means dressing like executives when selling to executives, softening the look as required when selling to non-executives, adding some high-fashion touches when selling to women, and otherwise accommodating dress to meet the perceptions and expectations of clients.

§ *Women of Color in the Corporate Workplace*

The dominance of European-based, English-speaking culture in the U.S. is beginning to slip, and it is probable that at some point in the 21st century Caucasians will become the new minority. Meanwhile, non-Caucasians have the challenge of conforming to current norms in the WASM (white Anglo-Saxon male)-dominated workplace while finding ways to celebrate their own cultural heritage and embrace their unique physical characteristics.

"Women of color" is a phrase used to designate races other than Caucasian, including African Americans, Asians, Hispanics, and Native Americans. Hair may be straight, curly, or kinky, and its colors cover a range of browns and blacks. Skin colors span peach through ebony. Although some of the remarks in this section apply to all women of color, they are particularly relevant to African American women.

In the past, women of color had to rely on makeup created for Caucasians. Initial attempts at formulating foundation for dark skin, however, resulted in products that were not much of an improvement. Fortunately, makeup is now available in blendable shades for darker skin, and image consultants who expect to have African American clients should become familiar with them. If the right shade of foundation is not available, two shades can be blended to match the complexion. Face powder similar in color to the foundation should be used. In *1001 Beauty Solutions* (Sourcebooks), Beth Barrick-Hickley also suggests using gray, black, or midnight blue eyeliner pencils instead of brown, which can accentuate an unflattering yellowish tint to the whites of the eyes.

In many cultures, hair is considered a woman's crowning glory. For decades African American women were taught that the standard for socially acceptable hair was the finely textured look of Western European origin. Toward this end, they used chemicals, heat, and various implements to relax, straighten, lighten, and otherwise alter their hair. Today, more African American women are appreciating the beauty of their own natural hair. However, if they want to make it in white corporate America, they are advised to choose styles that are not considered too ethnic or too non-conformist. A short, cropped hairdo, for example, would probably be considered neat, sophisticated, and attractive. On the other hand, cornrows or braids, while perfectly acceptable in more liberally-minded professions, would probably be considered too exotic for the executive suites of U.S. corporations.

While we are on the subject of hair, let's turn to the more delicate matter of body hair, specifically leg hair. African Americans and Latinos have a more relaxed attitude toward feminine leg hair than do whites in the U.S. Female body hair is a marker of sexuality, ethnicity, and "in-group" status for many cultures, according to William Stuart, director of undergraduate studies in anthropology at the University of Maryland, quoted in *The Washington Post*. But for whites of upper-middle class economic status, leg hair on a woman is a sign of poor grooming. For Caucasian and non-Caucasian women alike who aspire to climb the corporate ladder, clean-shaven legs are a requisite.

Many young, single women of all colors share the desire to dress in ways that express their sensuality at work. However, if their clothing or grooming is perceived as provocative, the assumption is that they are not career-minded and/or suitable for managerial and executive positions in the company. It may be unfair, but that's the reality. The corporate environment allows for a relatively narrow range of clothing for professionals, and "sexy" is not part of that range for women. Unfortunately, women of color have few role models in the corporate world to demonstrate what is appropriate. Image consultants of color can help fill in the gap by dressing in a professional manner when advising their clients of color.

When the concept of color seasons became popular in the 1980's, it was assumed that most women of color were winters. That assumption has proved to be false. Some women of color are winters and some are summers, with a blue or purple undertone to their skin. Some are springs and some are autumns, with a golden-yellow undertone to their skin.

Winters look best in cool, clear colors and summers in cool, soft colors. Springs look best in warm, clear colors, and autumns look best in warm, rich, muted colors. Hair color and makeup also have a cool or warm base. Using the right seasonal colors in clothing, makeup, and hair to enhance appearance is just as important to African American women as it is to Caucasian women. A good guide is *Women of Color* by Darlene Mathis, published by Ballantine Books.

What about body shapes? Although women of color come in all sizes and shapes, some African American women have larger derrieres and fuller figures in comparison to Caucasians. Because these physical characteristics do not conform to the ideals of beauty shown in magazines and movies, they can negatively influence a woman's image of herself and persuade her to overlook or put down her real beauty. A sensitive image consultant knows that the client who is guided to look her personal and professional best will be more likely to have positive feelings about herself.

How can a woman of color demonstrate ethnic pride and still fit into the corporate environment? In small doses, such as through the accessories she chooses. For example, her vest can be in a textile from her ancestral country, or she can select a pin, necklace, or other piece of jewelry of native origin. Summertime offers occasions to become a little bolder, particularly on business casual days, by mixing solid colors with textiles in indigenous ethnic patterns.

Notes

8 REFINING YOUR IMAGE CONSULTING BUSINESS

§ Taking Stock

Image consultants are creative people. They can't stand being in a rut for very long. If you've been in the business for a while, perhaps you've begun to feel somewhat restless, a little dissatisfied, a bit bored. It may be time to reassess what you are doing and where you are going.

Start by revisiting the business plan you filed away some time ago. Are you meeting the objectives you listed? Are you satisfied with the growth in your customer base? Are you making as much money as you'd like? Are there other directions you want to explore? Is it time to develop a new business plan?

§ Do More Business Seminars

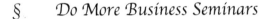

The fastest route to making more money in image consulting is to do seminars for corporations. In *Reinventing the Corporation,* John Naisbitt wrote that corporations spend nearly $60 billion a year on education and training. What percentage of this $60 billion are you making? I recommend that at least 50 percent of your income come from corporate seminars. For example, if your goal is to gross $60,000 a year, then $30,000 should come from corporate seminars. At $1,000 a day, you would present 30 seminars a year, or three a month. To achieve this you should make ten calls and send proposals to four companies a week. In preparing a proposal, determine the least amount of money you will accept, and then stick to that figure.

Business seminars not only improve your profitability but enhance your credentials as an authority and business leader and increase your visibility. Moreover, everyone in the audience becomes a potential client.

• *Who Can Afford You?* Look for a CEO who is image conscious. Find the companies that have training budgets. Call the human resources or personnel director of corporations involved in non-glamour industries such as

- banking
- insurance
- hotels
- real estate
- car dealerships
- computer sales
- health care
- transportation
- other retail sales
- temp agencies and employment agencies

Companies undergoing renovation or restructuring, associations, and government agencies are also possibilities.

Begin by selecting one industry and concentrating on calls and direct mail to companies within that industry. The Standard Rate and Data Service (SRDS) publishes business lists and direct list rates. In every city there are mailing lists to rent.

Read all the business newspapers in your area. Learn who is being promoted and who is in a position to hire you. Read all calendars of events. Attend at least one business or professional meeting a month.

- *Topics to Offer.* Some suggestions:

  - Polishing Your Company's Professional Image

  - Business Casual—What's Appropriate?

  - Business Etiquette and Protocol

  - First and Lasting Impressions—What Your Employees' Clothes, Grooming, and Body Language Communicate

  - How to Make Effective Presentations

- *The Proposal.* The proposal is an outline of the seminar you send to the prospective client. In addition, a page stating your qualifications may be included. A sample proposal on "Polishing Your Professional Image" for a hotel is on the following page. I've used variations of this outline for seminars at several hotels.

- *The Contract.* The contract may simply be in the form of a letter stating the terms agreed upon. Secure a 50 percent deposit to hold the date and include a cancellation clause.

- *Location.* If the seminar is to be held at other than the business location, select a hotel or restaurant with a pleasant ambiance. If possible, choose an informal setting to encourage group participation.

(SAMPLE PROPOSAL)

To: Peter Jones, General Manager, River Heights Hotel

From: Susan Smith, Better Image, LLC

Subject: Proposed Action Items and Agenda for Seminar, *Polishing Your Professional Image*

Preliminary Steps

1. Meet with Mr. Jones to ascertain a preliminary definition of the desired image for the River Heights Hotel.

2. Visit, as an anonymous outside observer, the various departments and take note of employee attire, body language, attitude, and knowledge of services offered.

3. Observe the staff at the Ridgeway Hotel to compare with the River Heights Hotel.

4. Meet with Mr. Jones to discuss my observations, finalize the definition of the desired image for the hotel, and receive input for final touches on the seminar.

Seminar Outline

I. First Impressions

- First 30 seconds are crucial
- How to create positive first impressions
- Position is your career, not just a job
- Competitive field requires that you stay on top

Polishing Your Professional Image   *Page 2*

II. Body Language

- Posture while standing, walking, sitting
- Developing a confident image
- Eye contact, smile, nervous mannerisms, chewing gum
- Non-verbal communication

III. Your Voice and What It Says about You

- 50% of your image
- Tone and diction
- Friendliness and enthusiasm

IV. You Are What Your Wear

- Define appropriate image
- Examples of correct and incorrect attire
- Psychology of color
- Power tools: shoes, briefcase, handbag, hosiery, pen, glasses, outerwear
- Developing a well-coordinated wardrobe on a budget

V. Presentation

Presentation from department or specialty store with examples of appropriate attire for men and women

VI. Grooming

- Hair
- Nails
- Skin
- Beard and moustache

Polishing Your Professional Image   *Page 3*

VII. Slide Presentation on Professional Wardrobe and Body
    Language

VIII. Question and Answer Period

Assignments for Follow-Up Session

1. Complete information on goals for image improvement.

2. Come to follow-up session with examples of appropriate and inappropriate attire and conversation.

3. Share your observations over the past week.

4. Review information on posture, carriage, voice, body language.

5. Discuss how participants have been able to incorporate information
gained from the seminar.

6. Check your closet for items you have questions about. Bring in
articles of clothing you are not sure about.

SAMPLE SEMINAR EVALUATION

1. I understood the goals of the seminar.
 ☐ Strongly agree ☐ Agree ☐ Disagree ☐ Strongly disagree ☐ Don't know

2. The overall objectives of the seminar were achieved.
 ☐ Strongly agree ☐ Agree ☐ Disagree ☐ Strongly disagree ☐ Don't know

3. There was adequate time to cover the material.
 ☐ Strongly agree ☐ Agree ☐ Disagree ☐ Strongly disagree ☐ Don't know

4. We should have additional training in this subject area.
 ☐ Strongly agree ☐ Agree ☐ Disagree ☐ Strongly disagree ☐ Don't know

	Did not like	Liked	Liked very much
5. Rate the speaker:			
Delivery/general speaking style	☐	☐	☐
Ability to relate to audience	☐	☐	☐
Content/message of material	☐	☐	☐
Adaptation of material to time allotted	☐	☐	☐
Pacing/speed of delivery	☐	☐	☐

6. Would you recommend this speaker? ☐ yes   ☐ no

 Why/Why not? _____

7. What did you like best about the seminar? _____

 _____

8. What did you like least about the seminar? _____

 _____

9. What additional training in this area would be helpful?

 _____

10. Please send me more information about this speaker. ☐

• *Using Visuals.* Use visual aids at the point in your presentation where they have the greatest impact. Tell the audience what they are going to see and what it illustrates. Make sure that you stand in a spot that does not block the audience's view, and speak toward the audience, not the visual. Know the visual well enough so that you don't have to ponder over it while you are talking. Coordinate or number the visual aids so that you use them smoothly in your presentation. **Have backup material in case something goes wrong.**

Other Tips

• It helps if you know something about your audience ahead of time. Ask your contact pertinent questions and, if possible, visit the company's quarters to observe.

• Have handouts to illustrate your points. Make it clear in the contract who will provide the copies. Ideally, the client is responsible for making photocopies from the master copies you provide ahead of time.

• At the outset of your presentation, state the goals and objectives and set the ground rules, such as holding questions until the end of a segment, when the break is scheduled, etc. Tell the audience what is happening throughout the presentation, and at the end of each segment, recap and summarize.

• Bring brochures and business cards.

§ Get the Support You Need

When you started your business, chances are you did everything yourself. If you are still doing everything yourself, consider delegating. Do those tasks that you enjoy and do well and be willing to pay others to do the rest. Surround yourself with competent and reliable associates.

Another aspect of support is getting what you need to revitalize your enthusiasm and get your creative juices flowing again. Take some continuing education courses. Keep in touch with other image consultants. Find out if there is an association of small business owners and attend meetings. If one doesn't exist, start one. You may want to consider joining an AICI chapter in your area.

Nurture your emotional life by spending quality time with friends and family. Every day, take some time to relax, reflect, and reconnect with your spirit.

§ Expand Your Client Services

You don't have to be in the business very long before you realize that positive image is an "inside" as well as an "outside" job. You may find it very satisfying to partner with others to offer a fuller range of services that consider your clients' holistic needs. For example, one of my most popular seminars is geared toward the maturing woman, featuring guest speakers on nutrition, exercise, hormone replacement therapy, psychology and even spirituality. In working with individual clients you may want to incorporate personality indicator testing. (See chapter 9.)

Keep your mind open. Let creative ideas surface, and be receptive to trying something new and different. When branching out into new areas, you may decide to gain exposure by initially offering free seminars to selected community groups. Send press releases—perhaps jointly with the community group—to ensure the seminars get local publicity.

§ Join the Technological Revolution

How are your computer skills? Are you surfing the Internet for the latest fashion news? Are you checking out the Web sites of other image consultants? Do you have a Web site of your own?

The successful 21st century image consultant is not only familiar with computer technology but uses it in her business. If you need to improve your computer skills, now is the time to hire a tutor or take an adult education class. There are word processing and graphics programs that will enable you to design your own brochures at a fraction of the price a graphics artist would charge. Who knows, you may end up designing your own Web page!

§ Surviving the Down Times

Image consulting is particularly vulnerable to the ups and downs of the general economy. When the economy is unstable or on the downswing, individuals and corporations alike react by reducing spending, cutting down on or eliminating goods and services other than those they consider essential. The savvy image consultant will recognize this and adapt to the changes in values and preferences that accompany a real or perceived economic downturn.

During economic downtimes you may need to lower your prices. If you've been accustomed to having your clients come to you, consider taking your services to them. Oblige your clients' desires for bargain prices by becoming an expert on discount and consignment shops. Know when there are sales at department and specialty stores. (This is where establishing good contacts among sales associates pays off.)

At the same time, offer seminars on investment dressing to your female clients, explaining that if 50 percent of the client's time is spent at work, then 50 percent of her clothing budget should be spent on clothes for work. Demonstrate that value, rather than initial price, can be more economical in the long run by taking into account the cost per wearing formula: cost per wearing equals garment cost divided by the total number of wearings.

To stimulate ideas for expanding your customer base, reread the previous chapters of this book. Also, this may be the time to actively explore establishing partnerships with professionals in other disciplines, as described above. Treat this period as an opportunity to plumb your creative depths. You may come up with ideas you would never have thought of when it was "business as usual." For example, AFI's Home Study Program was born out of the economic recession in the early 1990's during which time I explored ways to provide a flexible, less expensive alternative to classroom instruction that would continue to include one-on-one mentoring.

During economic slow periods you may want to offer your services *pro bono* to a woman's shelter, welfare-to-work program, or senior citizens' center. Not only will this help keep your spirits up by helping others, it will reinforce the fact that there is real social value in your chosen work. Finally, take heart. This situation is only temporary. The economy will rebound and demand for your services will be greater than ever.

9 PERSONALITY TYPES

§ *Behavioral Preferences*

This chapter is not about the personality types you learn about in a class on wardrobe line and style—classic, sporty/natural, romantic, ingenue, gamin. It is about personality types based on the theories of the late psychologist/psychiatrist Carl Jung and subsequently refined by others.

According to Jung and his successors, people exhibit preferences in how they are energized, how they gather information, how they react in situations, and how they make decisions. *Extroverts,* for example, are energized more by the outside world, while *Introverts* are stimulated by the internal world. In gathering information, *Sensors* rely more on hard evidence perceived through the senses, while *Intuitives* rely more on ideas and "gut feelings." *Feelers* tend to make decisions based on emotion and *Thinkers* through thought processing. *Perceivers* prefer to keep things open-ended and consequently put off making decisions, while *Judgers* make decisions relatively quickly because they want closure.

Of course, all of us are stimulated by thought and ideas as well as by people and events. We rely on our senses and on our intuition. We both think and feel, make plans and put things off . Nevertheless, we tend to have a preferred mode in each behavioral category -- an inclination that comes to the forefront in the majority of situations.

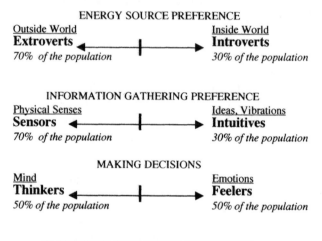

ENERGY SOURCE PREFERENCE

Outside World   Inside World
Extroverts   **Introverts**
70% of the population   *30% of the population*

INFORMATION GATHERING PREFERENCE

Physical Senses   Ideas, Vibrations
Sensors   **Intuitives**
70% of the population   *30% of the population*

MAKING DECISIONS

Mind   Emotions
Thinkers   **Feelers**
50% of the population   *50% of the population*

CLOSURE OR OPEN-ENDED PREFERENCE

Closure   Open-Ended
Judgers   **Perceivers**
55% of the population   *45% of the population*

Knowing about behavioral preferences is important to understanding ourselves as well as understanding those with whom we interact. When we are aware of personality types we are less likely to misinterpret the behavior and responses of others. We become more willing to allow others to see things through their own lens, without feeling they are being disagreeable, obstinate, elusive, or stupid. As image consultants, we can adjust our approaches to clients and become more effective communicators, educators, and marketers.

§ *Test Yourself*

The process of learning about personality types begins with learning about one's own. Start by doing the sample exercises in the following pages. In each of the four behavioral areas there is a set of statements. Each statement can be completed by one of two possible responses. Choose the response that best describes you **most of the time**. If you can't relate to either response, leave the statement blank. If you feel that both responses apply equally, check both.

When you have completed your responses in a behavioral area, add the number of checks in each column. The column with the most checks indicates a tendency toward that behavioral characteristic and the strength of that tendency. Your personality type is a composite of the strongest behavioral characteristics in all four areas.

INTROVERT (I) VERSUS EXTROVERT (E)

As social beings we all need people, but for EXTROVERTED TYPES, getting out and socializing with others is vital to their mental health. The outer world of people and activities provides energy and stimulation for extroverts. Approachable and easy to get to know, they often have a wide circle of friends. They communicate their opinions and ideas easily and are likely to act first and think about it later. They prefer to work with others rather than alone. There are over twice as many extroverts as there are introverts in the general population.

While all of us can benefit from taking time for ourselves, withdrawing from the outside world and going inward is an absolute requirement for INTROVERTED TYPES. They retreat into thoughts and ideas to recharge their batteries, and they must do it frequently. Introverts don't make quick decisions; they must think about

- continued -

INTROVERT (I) VERSUS EXTROVERT (E)

1. *I am inclined to recharge my batteries when I am*   by myself ___   with people ____

2. *People I don't know are*   easy to approach ___   hard to approach ___

3. *I am more stimulated by*   the inner world of thoughts & ideas ___   the outer world of people & events ___

4. *I usually agree to do something*   after reflecting on it ___   quickly (sometimes regretting it later) ___

5. *When it comes to gossip I tend to be*   among the last to know ___   among the first to know ___

6. *Before I make an important phone call I usually*   write down/rehearse what I'll say ___   I have a general idea of what I'll say ___

7. *People think I am*   hard to get to know ___   easy to get to know ___

8. *Most of the time I prefer*   to work by myself ___   to work with others ___

9. *I have*   a few close friends ___   lots of friends ___

10. *I tend to be*   reserved ___   outgoing ___

I ____   E ____

it first. Often quiet and reserved, introverts can be hard to get to know. They usually limit their circle to a few close friends, and they prefer to work alone or with a small number of people.

The tendency toward either introversion or extroversion occurs on a continuum. A person whose introversion is less pronounced and who is also a strong feeling type (IF) is often mistaken for an extrovert. The determinant is the person's primary energy source—does it come from the outer world or the inner world?

INTUITIVE (N) VERSUS SENSOR (S)

1. *I prefer to work with*	possibilities ___	hard data ___
2. *I am more interested in*	what's around the bend ___	the present ___
3. *I'd describe myself as*	creative ___	practical ___
4. *I prefer to*	think it up ___	do it ___
5. *I am intrigued by*	fac t patterns ___	facts ___
6. *I'd rather be*	daydreaming ___	accomplishing ___
7. *I'm inclined toward*	the figurative ___	the literal ___
8. *I prefer*	general guidelines ___	specific instructions ___
9. *My attitude is best described*	"it's exciting to find new ways to do things" ___	"if it ain't broke, don't fix it" ___
10. *I am more*	imaginative ___	realistic ___
11. *I like to*	improvise ___	follow directions ___
12. *Some might criticize*	my head's in the clouds ___	I'm wedded to routine ___
13. *I'd rather work in*	research ___	development ___

N ___   **S** ___

INTUITIVE TYPES are conceptual, big-picture, future-oriented people, intrigued by possibilities. They value ideas over hard facts, the imaginative over the practical, the whole over the parts. Intuitives must create. They are not content to follow someone else's instructions, and the ideas of other people are just starting points for building.

- continued -

their own. When presented with hard data they will automatically look for patterns, associations, connections, purpose. Intuitives often work in energy bursts, followed by slack periods. If they are INTPs ((Introverted, Intuitive, Thinking, Perceivers) they may prefer to work with the purely theoretical.

SENSING TYPES comprise 70 percent of the population. They are rooted in the here-and-now of physical reality, preferring facts over ideas and the practical over the fanciful. They are frequently detail-oriented and place great value on order and precision—consider the auditor crunching numbers on his calculator, the neurosurgeon wielding a scalpel, the skater doing figure eights, the aviator landing on the deck of an aircraft carrier. Sensors prefer action to talk, doing to dreaming. They take pleasure in movement and in what is perceived through the senses. There is great variety among sensors, depending on how their sensing preference is integrated with other behavioral characteristics.

THINKER (T) VERSUS FEELER (F)

THINKING TYPES focus first on the truth and logic of a situation rather than on the people involved. They need to know why. Thinkers value clear-mindedness and objectivity. They look for inconsistencies and zero-in on what needs to be fixed, whether it's a situation, an event, a project, or a presentation, and they may be perceived as overly critical. Thinkers may not show emotion easily and can come off as cold and unfeeling when in reality they are capable of great feeling, particularly where fairness and justice are involved.

FEELING TYPES tend to consider the welfare of people first, focusing on their values and needs. They are quick to praise, and, in turn, like to be praised. Feelers seek agreement and look for ways that everyone can benefit. They look for and promote the positive. Compassionate and caring, feelers project a warm, friendly attitude. Sometimes their empathetic manner is misconstrued as an invitation to greater intimacy than they are prepared for. Some feeling types may have trouble asserting themselves and may allow themselves to be taken advantage of.

- continued -

THINKER (T) VERSUS FEELER (F)

1. *I am inclined to be*   objective ___   subjective ___

2. *I am more*   analytical ___   sentimental ___

3. *I make most decisions*   with my head ___   with my heart ___

4. *I would probably be described as*   fair-minded ___   warm and caring ___

5. *I am apt to*   spot the flaws ___   praise the effort ___

6. *I lean toward*   justice ___   leniency ___

7. *I would describe myself as more*   reasonable ___   emotional ___

8. *My decisions tend to be based on*   thinking things through ___   what I feel ___

9. *I see myself as more*   neutral ___   compassionate ___

10. *Some might accuse me of being too*   critical ___   soft-hearted ___

11. *In problem solving, I focus on*   the good of the organization ___   people's feelings ___

12. *I put a premium on*   competence ___   harmony ___

13. *I prefer*   honest feedback from someone I respect ___   praise ___

14. *It is most important to*   do a thorough job ___   reach agreement ___

T ___   **F** ___

JUDGER (J) VERSUS PERCEIVER (P)

1. *I prefer to*   have things settled ___   keep my options open ___

2. *Deadlines are*   to be met ___   guidelines ___

3. *I am more uneasy*   when things are incomplete ___   complete ___

4. *I consider myself more*   organized ___   flexible ___

5. *My approach is more*   deliberate ___   impulsive ___

6. *This describes my work habits*   plan and do ___   last minute rush ___

7. *This scenario is more familiar*   make a list, complete the list ___   make a list, change the list, lose the list ___

8. *I am usually*   on time ___   late ___

9. *I am more comfortable*   after a decision ___   before a decision ___

10. *I prefer*   having a routine ___   keeping things flexible ___

11. *I tend to*   make up my mind quickly ___   put things off ___

12. *My philosophy is*   let's decide now ___   let's wait and see ___

J ___   **P ___**

- continued -

JUDGERS require closure. They need to get things done. They like organization and structure—tools that give judging types a sense of security that things will get done. These are the people who plan the agendas, figure out the operational details, and come up with the timetables. Judgers work hard and are more subject to stress than perceivers. Workaholics tend to be Judgers.

PERCEIVERS are flexible and spontaneous. They like to experience life as it happens. They don't worry about how they are going to get something done, they just do it as they go along. Perceiving types prefer an open-ended, "let's just see what happens" approach. Because they don't close off their options early, perceivers are the explorers and the inventors. Usually they are not good with details, and they may lack a keen awareness of time, often waiting until the final hour to complete a task or showing up late for engagements.

§ *Finding Your Personality Type*

Your personality type is a composite of the strongest behavioral characteristics in the four areas. There are 16 combinations of these behavioral characteristics, resulting in 16 personality types:

ENFJ Extroverted-Intuitive-Feeling-Judging
5% of the U.S. population
ENFP Extroverted-Intuitive-Feeling-Perceiving
5% of the U.S. population
ENTJ Extroverted-Intuitive-Thinking-Judging
5% of the U.S. population
ENTP Extroverted-Intuitive-Thinking-Perceiving
5% of the U.S. population

INFJ Introverted-Intuitive-Feeling-Judging
1% of the U.S. population
INFP Introverted-Intuitive-Feeling-Perceiving
1% of the U.S. population
INTJ Introverted-Intuitive-Thinking-Judging
1% of the U.S. population
INTP Introverted-Intuitive-Thinking-Perceiving
1% of the U.S. population

ESFJ Extroverted-Sensing-Feeling-Judging
13% of the U.S. population
ESFP Extroverted-Sensing-Feeling-Perceiving
13% of the U.S. population
ESTJ Extroverted-Sensing-Thinking-Judging
13% of the U.S. population
ESTP Extroverted-Sensing-Thinking-Perceiving
13% of the U.S. population

ISFJ Introverted-Sensing-Feeling-Judging
6% of the U.S. population
ISFP Introverted-Sensing-Feeling-Perceiving
6% of the U.S. population
ISTJ Introverted-Sensing-Thinking-Judging
6% of the U.S. population
ISTP Introverted-Sensing-Thinking-Perceiving
6% of the U.S. population

Source of Percentages: Keirsey & Bates

It is interesting to speculate that one of the reasons we are so image conscious is because of the influence of the Sensors in the population, particularly Extroverted Sensors (ES). Although all of us get information through our senses, ES types rely on their senses as their primary channels for gathering information, which then becomes the basis for forming judgments. In general, they prefer definitive boundaries and rules. The polar opposite to ES types are Introverted Intuitives (IN), who comprise only four percent of the population. IN types are more likely to ponder the information they receive rather than make snap judgments. They place more importance on their intuition as opposed to what they see and hear.

The following scenario is illustrative of how personality types can affect your work as an image consultant. Mary Jones was relieved when the image seminar she presented to a group of certified public accountants was finally over. She was convinced that it had not gone well. The previous month she had given essentially the same seminar to a group of insurance sales people and they had been receptive and enthusiastic. But the accountants just sat there, polite, but as far as Mary could tell, bored. She had provided each member of the audience with an outline, and at one point she deviated from it, searching for ways to perk up the accountants' interest. However, this tactic just seemed to distress them.

What Mary, an ENFP (Extroverted-Intuitive-Feeling-Perceiver), did not realize was that she had walked into a room filled with ISTJs (Introverted-Sensing-Thinking-Judgers). Their personality types could not have been more dissimilar from hers, unlike the personalities of the sales people, who shared Mary's EF (Extroverted Feeling) traits.

If Mary had understood about personality types she could have made some minor adjustments in her style of delivery to the accountants. She would have realized that their lack of emotional response and occasional curt questions did not mean that they had not appreciated the seminar. In actuality, the accountants thought it went rather well, and would have been surprised to learn that Mary assumed it was a failure.

It's easier to identify individual behaviors than it is to come up with a standardized description of the personality type that results from combining behaviors. This is partly because of the possible variations in individual behavioral areas depending on where the person is on the continuum in each area. In addition, there are many other factors involved in forming personality, including family and cultural influences. Consequently, you may find that a description of your personality type has some characteristics that apply to you and some that do not.

The brief profiles on the following pages suggest the kinds of jobs suitable for each personality type. However, they do not necessarily indicate the personality type of a person employed in that profession. For example, an INTP is likely to be in his element if he is a philosopher, scientist, mathematician, or logician. But that does not mean all philosophers, scientists, mathematicians and logicians are invariably INTPs.

INTUITIVES:

ENFJ   People-oriented, popular, responsive to people's feelings. Verbally adept. Likes to facilitate others. Good group leader. Responsible and organized. Inspired toward change and new ideas. *Includes executives, ministers, teachers, therapists, sales people, actors.*

ENFP   Popular with others. Flexible and adaptable. Relies on improvisational skills. Has many creative ideas but lacks interest in details involved in implementation. Good host. *Includes sales people, politicians, screenwriters, performers.*

INFJ
Reserved. Compassionate and sensitive to others. Respected for their principles. Interested in the common good. Imaginative and insightful. *Includes poets, novelists, songwriters, ministers, therapists.*

INFP
Reserved and idealistic, with a strong system of values. Adaptable, but impatient with details. Not likely to go into business. *Includes ministers, missionaries, psychiatrists, psychologists, college-level teachers.*

ENTJ
Take-charge types who are policy and goal-oriented. Good visualizers. Strong organizational skills. *Includes many types of executives and leaders.*

ENTP
Gregarious, enthusiastic, open-minded. Easy to get along with. Innovative. Dislikes routine and tends to neglects the details. *Includes teachers, politicians, sales people.*

INTJ
Quiet, reserved, introspective. Good at strategizing, proving, classifying, summarizing. Approaches projects with an overall vision. Works best alone or with a small number of people. *Includes scientific researchers, human engineers, executives.*

INTP
Shy, precise, tenacious. Architect of ideas. *Includes philosophers, scientists, mathematicians, logicians.*

SENSORS:

ESFJ
Very sociable. Nurturer who is duty- and service-oriented. Likes to work with things that

visibly affect people's lives. Emotional. *Includes sales people, supervisors, administrators, coaches, teachers, ministers.*

ESFP   Outgoing, charming, fun, generous. Verbal. Good at entertaining. *Includes sales people, public relations persons, social workers, elementary school teachers, performers.*

ISFJ   Devoted and loyal. Traditional. Dislikes change. Status-conscious. Follows rules, regulations, and procedures to the letter. Hard worker. Service-oriented. *Includes middle managers and administrators, secretaries, librarians, doctors, nurses, teachers.*

ISFP   Kind , empathetic, impulsive. Uninterested in academia. Very sense-oriented. Frequently in the fine arts. *Includes composers, painters, dancers.*

ESTJ   Conservative. Tradition, order, rituals, and following procedures are very important. Dependable and consistent. Can be intolerant of different views. Involved in community affairs. *Includes business managers and administrators.*

ESTP   Charming, clever, and popular. Observant and resourceful. A natural negotiator. Initiates actions but bored with details. Some like living on the edge. *Includes sales and advertising people, professional athletes, gamblers, soldiers of fortune.*

ISTJ   Quiet, serious, practical and patient. Sensible, reliable, efficient, and thorough, with a deep sense of honor. Detail-oriented. *Includes auditors, accountants, bank examiners, morticians, legal secretaries, and high school teachers in business, the physical sciences, home economics, and physical education.*

| ISTP | Impulsive and easily bored. Can be insubordinate to others' rules and schedules. Enjoys working with tools. Good at solving practical problems. Some types crave excitement through physical adventure. *Includes mechanics, race car drivers, surgeons, sculptors, weapons experts, pilots, mountain climbers.* |

§ *What about Image Consultants?*

In general, Extroverted Feeling (EF) types are the most likely to be drawn to image consulting. Their favorite part of the job would be the people contact. Their warm, outgoing, sympathetic personalities are particularly suited for helping people improve themselves, and they enjoy working with large and small groups. Because much of the preparatory work and business aspects are done alone, EFs have to make a special effort to connect with others when they are not involved with clients.

Of the 16 behavioral combinations, ENFJs and ESFJs are most suited to be image consultants. (This author is an ENFJ.) ENFPs and ESFPs often have flair and a great rapport with people and may be attracted to image consulting. However, they must be willing to discipline their free-wheeling tendencies if they expect to earn a living in the profession. Perhaps the major difference between an Extroverted Sensor (ES) and an Extroverted Intuitive (EN) is that the ES type would concentrate on the performance aspects of the job while the EN would also be interested in finding new ways to present things and new services to offer.

INFJs would probably be comfortable in delivering services to individuals or small groups in intimate settings. They would be less bothered by the solitary work the profession requires. A shy INFJ may prefer to work with an extroverted partner.

Least likely to become image consultants are the thinking (as opposed to feeling) types, particularly ISTJs, ISTPs, ESTPs, and INTPs. An ENTJ could be intrigued by the possibilities and variety involved in the work. This personality type might come across as more reserved and critical than an ENFJ.

§   *Where to Get More Information*

Career counselors use personality indicators with their clients to help in identifying the jobs for which they are best suited. Corporations, universities, and government agencies use them to improve working relationships among employees. Image consultants can use them to provide an additional service to help clients improve their self-understanding and communications skills.

Perhaps the best known test of personality types is the **Myers-Briggs Type Indicator (MBTI)**, available from Psychologists Press, Inc., 3803 E. Bayshore Road, Palo Alto, CA 94303; web site, *www.cpp-db.com.* The MBTI is much more extensive than the sample contained in this chapter. To improve the accuracy of the indicator, the questions on the MBTI are not presented separately by behavioral category but are mixed so that a key is required for scoring. Isabel Myers-Briggs has written many books on the applications of the MBTI, including *Gifts Differing* (Consulting Psychologists Press, 1982).

Another personality type indicator is the **Keirsey Temperament Sorter,** which is contained in the book *Please Understand Me,* by David Keirsey and Marilyn Bates (1978), Prometheus Books, Box 2748, Del Mar, CA 92014; phone 619-632-1575. A list of questions from the Temperament Sorter are available on the Internet at *www.Keirsey.com.*

It is important to remember that the purpose of personality typing is to increase understanding, not to limit or pigeonhole. Making use of personality typing indicators is somewhat analogous to color analysis. You know the color theories and you use them to evaluate your clients, but you soon find that each individual is unique. Sometimes the theories clearly apply; sometimes their application is not so clear cut.

"Type is just one of many markers—age, sex, ethnic and religious background, even geography—that help us predict other people's behavior," O.W. Lacy wrote in the preface to *Gifts Differing.* "One's appropriate type is not a cell from which there is no escape, but a home ground from which one can venture forth to live life more fully."

Notes

10 RESOURCES

IMAGE CONSULTANT TRAINING

ACADEMY OF FASHION & IMAGE (AFI)
Brenda York-McDaniel
   19860 N. 85th Ave.
   Peoria, AZ 85382
      Toll Free: 800-450-5545
      Phone: 623-572-8719
      Fax: 623-572-2954
      E-mail: brenda@afiyork.com
      website: www.afiyork.com

Complete image consultant training leading to certification. Mentoring included. Self-paced home study program usually takes three to six months. Tuition is $1,800 - $2,000. Five-day classroom program costs $3,000. May be paid in installments. Director has 25 years as an image consultant and 17 years as a trainer/mentor. References available.

About Brenda York-McDaniel

Brenda is the director of the Academy of Fashion and Image, which she founded in 1983 to train prospective image consultants and provide continuing education for experienced consultants. The curriculum she developed has been continuously expanded and updated and is now available through a home study program.

An image consultant since 1976, Brenda also designs and delivers corporate seminars on positive image enhancement to industries that deal extensively with the public, such as retail, hotel, hospitality, insurance, and health care, as well as civic and professional organizations.

Brenda founded the first international organization to promote professionalism in the image industry. She has appeared on television and radio and has been featured in newspapers such as *The Washington Post, Chicago Tribune, N.Y. Daily News, USA Today, Wall Street Journal,* and *West Palm Beach Post,* in addition to numerous magazines and periodicals, including *Changing Times, Entrepreneur, Glamour, Mademoiselle, Newsweek, People Magazine, Success, U.S. News and World Report, The Winning Style,* and *101 Best Businesses.*

website: www.afiyork.com